CULTURES OF THE WORLD
Turkmenistan

Cavendish Square
New York

Published in 2021 by Cavendish Square Publishing, LLC
243 5th Avenue, Suite 136, New York, NY 10016
Copyright © 2021 by Cavendish Square Publishing, LLC

Third Edition

Website: cavendishsq.com

This publication represents the opinions and views of the author based on his or her personal experience, knowledge, and research. The information in this book serves as a general guide only. The author and publisher have used their best efforts in preparing this book and disclaim liability rising directly or indirectly from the use and application of this book.

All websites were available and accurate when this book was sent to press.

Library of Congress Cataloging-in-Publication Data

Names: Knowlton, MaryLee, 1946– author. | Nevins, Debbie, author.
Title: Turkmenistan / MaryLee Knowlton and Debbie Nevins.
Description: Third edition. | New York : Cavendish Square Publishing, 2021.
 | Series: Cultures of the world | Includes bibliographical references
 and index.
Identifiers: LCCN 2020042523 | ISBN 9781502658760 (library binding) | ISBN
 9781502658777 (ebook)
Subjects: LCSH: Turkmenistan—Juvenile literature.
Classification: LCC DK933 .K58 2021 | DDC 958.5—dc23
LC record available at https://lccn.loc.gov/2020042523

Writers: MaryLee Knowlton; Debbie Nevins, third edition
Editor, third edition: Debbie Nevins
Designer, third edition: Jessica Nevins
Picture Researcher, third edition: Jessica Nevins

PICTURE CREDITS

Find us on

CONTENTS

TURKMENISTAN TODAY

TURKMENISTAN IS OFTEN CALLED A "HERMIT NATION," A secretive, closed society. It's a nation in Central Asia, which is already a little-known region to many Westerners, and the country's isolation only adds to its mystery. Closer examination reveals a curious authoritarian culture that foreigners might not understand. However, real people live real lives in this distant, strange land. To them, it isn't strange; it's simply home.

Turkmenistan is a relatively new nation, carved out of the desert lands of Central Asia by the Soviets in the early 20th century. It was forced to spend most of that century as a communist Soviet republic, during which time the people had Russian language and culture imposed upon them. It was finally liberated when the Soviet Union collapsed in the early 1990s.

The Turkmen culture itself is quite ancient, born of nomadic peoples whose way of life harmonized with the land and the seasons. It was a lifestyle that worked well for many centuries until invading powers forced the people to adjust to new ways that worked against nature and against their heritage.

Crowds celebrate Independence Day outside of the presidential palace in Ashgabat, the capital of Turkmenistan.

Upon gaining independence in 1991, Turkmenistan could have tried to recoup that heritage, but times had changed, and perhaps too much damage had been done. Since becoming its own country, Turkmenistan has been under complete totalitarian rule. First, it was ruled by Saparmurat Niyazov, a man who called himself Turkmenbashi, the "Father (or Leader) of all Turkmen." Under his increasingly bizarre leadership, the economy faltered and the country became more isolated from its neighbors and other potential allies. In his time, he was regarded as one of the world's most totalitarian, despotic, and repressive dictators. He built absolute power through what is called a "cult of personality," a phenomenon in which unscrupulous leaders are idolized in a culture of hero-worship. This doesn't happen by accident; state-supported propaganda works insidiously to build an aura of invincibility around the leader. Indeed, the Turkmenistani people came to regard Turkmenbashi as almost a god, which seems to be the way he regarded himself.

He used his absolute power to impose his peculiar ideas on the populace. For example, he mandated that a book he had authored be the country's primary educational and life guidance text. He closed many hospitals around the country to compel people to come to Ashgabat, the capital city, for all their health-care needs. He slashed pension benefits to the elderly but spent lavishly to construct hundreds of enormous, gleaming white marble buildings in Ashgabat.

When Niyazov died in 2006, any hopes for a return to a normal government were quickly dashed. His successor, Gurbanguly Berdimuhamedov, quickly built his own cult of personality and continued on in the authoritarian manner.

What the Turkmenistani people actually think of him, or of their government in general, is hard to gauge. For one thing, no freedom of expression is allowed. Dissidents are dealt with very harshly, which intimidates and suppresses others. People who live in such places tend to forget how to think for themselves. With no opposing viewpoints, a totally state-controlled media (and absolutely no foreign media), a tightly censored internet, and virtually no exposure to other cultures, people lose the ability to formulate critical thoughts. It's simply a survival mechanism, and it is alive and well in Turkmenistan.

Berdimuhamedov's intense control over his nation has created a very stable country in an unstable region. To its southeast, Turkmenistan borders Afghanistan, one of the world's most volatile, unpredictable nations. That battle-weary country, torn by decades of civil war and outside interference, is ruled more by local warlords than by its national government. Parts of Afghanistan are largely under the control of the Taliban, a militant Islamic fundamentalist political organization known for its extremely strict interpretation of Islam. It's also well known for its brutality, particularly toward women.

Turkmenistan is an officially neutral country. It does not participate in any sort of regional political alliances or security arrangements. The nation's much-vaunted neutrality contributes to its isolation. It also means that Turkmenistan has to rely solely on its own power to prevent Afghanistan's insurgency from crossing its border.

Like all of its Central Asian neighbors, Turkmenistan is a primarily Muslim country. However, its government is secular, and it works vigorously to prevent any expression of Islamic fundamentalism from gaining power. The tense

Guards stand at attention at the base of the Monument of Neutrality, now in its new location on the outskirts of Ashgabat.

situation in Afghanistan—and in some other countries in the region, where fundamentalism is growing—is therefore a matter of great concern to the Berdimuhamedov regime.

Since leaving the Soviet Union, Turkmenistan has worked to cast off a century of Russian influence and reclaim its own culture. In this, it largely shares the history and heritage of most Central Asian peoples. Their Turkic languages, nomadic lifestyles, traditional dress and diets, and folk arts have much in common. However, in embracing its own Turkmen culture, the leadership has shown a strong tendency to idealize, mythologize, and glorify the past.

The people of Turkmenistan are said to be warm and welcoming in general, though few foreigners have had the ability to really get to know them. Personal liberty is severely limited, and those few who speak out in opposition to the government have been known to simply disappear. The international organization Human Rights Watch reported in 2019 that "the government punishes any kind of independent political or religious expression. Access to information is strictly controlled and no independent monitoring groups are allowed. The government keeps everyone, especially families of prisoners, in a constant state of fear. Torture is widespread and the media is heavily censored."

That said, Turkmenistan is far from the least happy place on earth. The 2020 World Happiness Report ranked the country at number 87 out of 156 countries, in which number 1 (Finland) was the happiest and number 156 (South Sudan) was the least happy. Turkmenistan's neighbor Afghanistan ranked a dismal number 154 that year. The report is an annual publication of the United Nations Sustainable Development Solutions Network.

Happiness, of course, is hard to measure. In this case, happiness is regarded as an expression of a population's general well-being. The results of this survey are based on six key variables: GDP per capita, social support, life expectancy, freedom to make life choices, generosity, and perceptions of corruption. (Other international organizations attempt to quantify the same concept using other indicators.) Since some of the data is based on answers to polling questions, it reflects individuals' perceptions of their own life experience.

To the extent that international rankings can evaluate a people's well-being, Turkmenistan can be said to be somewhere in the middle. Judging by how the nation portrays itself to the world, however, it seems to be the happiest place on earth. The truth, however, is far more complicated than that.

GEOGRAPHY

The rough landscape of Nisa, Turkmenistan, lies close to the country's border with Iran.

1

TURKMENISTAN IS THE SECOND-largest nation in Central Asia, the vast expanse that lies east of Europe and west of China. It's one of the five "'Stans" that are located there, between Russia to the north and India to the south. *Stan* is a Persian word that means "land of," and Kazakhstan, Kyrgyzstan, Tajikistan, Turkmenistan, and Uzbekistan are named for the ethnic peoples who live in them. (There are other 'Stans, some more familiar to Westerners—including Afghanistan and Pakistan—but strictly speaking, they are not in Central Asia.)

Slightly larger than the state of California, Turkmenistan is technically landlocked—that is, it has no access to the ocean. However, it does have coastline on the Caspian Sea, the world's largest inland body of water. Other nations that border this ancient body of water are Azerbaijan, Iran, Kazakhstan, and Russia.

Turkmenistan shares its southern borders with Iran and Afghanistan. Uzbekistan lies to the north and east, and Kazakhstan lies to the north. These borders did not exist until the early 20th century. The Soviets, in their takeover of Central Asia, found it politically expedient to divide

In area, Turkmenistan is the second-largest country in Central Asia. However, its population of about 6 million is the smallest in the region because so much of its land is uninhabitable desert. About half the population lives in and around the capital city of Ashgabat.

the lands into various republics as part of the newly founded Union of Soviet Socialist Republics (USSR) confederation.

From 1925 to 1991, Turkmenistan was the Turkmen Soviet Socialist Republic, a constituent republic of the Soviet Union. The residents of today's Turkmenistan and its neighbors had nothing to say about the matter while their nations were being brought into official existence by the Soviet leadership. The people living in much of Central Asia had been mostly nomadic, and establishing borders cut many of them off from either their summer or their winter pastures and forced them to change their lifestyles.

Almost all of Turkmenistan is desert or steppe. The sands of the Karakum Desert (also spelled Kara-Kum or Gara-Gum) cover 70 percent of the nation's total landmass of 188,407 square miles (488,000 square kilometers). Most of the people live in oasis settlements in the southern shadow of the Kopet-Dag mountain range or along Turkmenistan's three main rivers: the Murgab, the Tedzhen, and the Amu Darya.

The Amu Darya marks much of the border between Uzbekistan, in the foreground, and Turkmenistan, on the other side. *Darya* is the Persian word for "river."

THE LARGEST INLAND SEA—OR LAKE?

The Caspian Sea is the largest inland body of water in the world. It's much bigger than Lake Superior, the greatest of the North American Great Lakes and the second-largest lake in the world after the Caspian. For comparison, the Caspian measures around 750 miles (1,200 km) from north to south, and is about 200 miles (320 km) wide. It covers around 149,200 square miles (386,400 sq km) in area. Lake Superior, in contrast, measures only 160 miles (258 km) from north to south, and is 350 miles (563 km) wide from east to west. It covers 31,700 square miles (82,100 sq km).

However, is the comparison even valid? Unlike Lake Superior, or any of the Great Lakes, the Caspian is not a freshwater body but a salt lake. Then there's its name—it's not Caspian Lake after all, but the Caspian Sea. So which is it—a lake or a sea? As it turns out, that's a question geologists have long struggled with and never quite settled.

About 11 million years ago—relatively recent in geologic time—the Caspian was linked to the ocean by way of the Sea of Azov, the Black Sea, the Aegean Sea, and the Mediterranean Sea. At that point, it was unquestionably a sea. Over time, the rising landforms of Asia and Europe slowly isolated the saltwater Caspian in a large hollow that is around 72 feet (22 m) below sea level.

The depth of the sea varies greatly, from a shallow 12 to 20 feet (3.7 to 6.1 meters) in the north to a maximum depth of 3,360 feet (1,025 m). There is also wide variation in the water's salinity, or salt content. In the cooler north, where great Russian freshwater rivers such as the Volga and Vistula flow into the Caspian Sea, the salt content is low. In the subtropical south, where evaporation occurs at a much faster rate, the salinity level is much higher. On average, the Caspian's salinity is about one-third that of ocean water.

With 1,098 miles (1,768 km) of Caspian Sea coastline, Turkmenistan has the second-longest amount of coastline on the sea, after Kazakhstan's 1,181 miles (1900 km).

STEPPE

The Russian word *step*, which describes the lands of Siberia, has become a part of the English language, spelled "steppe." It refers to a semiarid area of land where grass grows or once did. Steppes fall into three categories. Wooded steppe receives more than 16 inches (41 centimeters) of precipitation annually, enough to support tree life. Tillable steppe is made of fertile black soil and gets 10 to 15 inches (25 to 38 cm) of annual rainfall. Native grasses—ideal for grazing livestock—thrive, and irrigation allows for continuing productive agriculture as it does in the wheat belts of the United States and Russia. Finally, there is the non-tillable steppe, which receives less than 10 inches (25 cm) of rain per year.

In Turkmenistan the land generally falls into the third and least hospitable category of steppe. Non-tillable, or semi-desert, conditions prevail. The lives and livelihoods of the people of Turkmenistan have been shaped by the adaptations they have made to the demands of this challenging environment.

THE KARAKUM DESERT

The Karakum Desert is called the Garagum in Turkmen, meaning "Black Sand." Stretching 500 miles (805 km) from east to west and 300 miles (483 km) from north to south, its 135,000 square miles (349,650 sq km) constitute 70 to 80 percent of the entire land area of Turkmenistan. Its southern border is formed by the Kopet-Dag mountains. To its northeast lies another desert, the Kyzyl Kum (also spelled Kyzylkum). The little water that is found there naturally flows from the Hindu Kush mountains, which lie to the south of the desert, where the Murgab and Tedzhen Rivers provide irrigation water.

The Karakum has three distinct parts: the northern, southeastern, and central parts of the desert. Each has its own climate. However, throughout the entire region, summers are generally hot and very dry. The northern part of the desert is called the Trans-Unguz Karakum, where the summers are the coolest—ranging from 79 to 82 degrees Fahrenheit (26 to 28 degrees Celsius)—and the rainfall the scarcest—only 2.75 inches (7 cm) a year. The average winter temperature is 25°F (-4°C), but in the Trans-Unguz Karakum, and in the desert as a whole, it can fluctuate more than 50°F (28°C) on any given day.

Animals and plants are not plentiful in the Karakum, but they are varied. In April, the desert blooms, and for a few short weeks, it is alive with flowering plants whose bright reds, yellows, and oranges enliven the landscape. Fruit thrives in the oasis and irrigated areas and is especially plentiful in the fall.

Oases located near both the city and province of Mary and the Tedzhen region have made these areas critical to Turkmenistan's cotton crop. Their commercial legacy can be traced back several centuries. They were once important stops for traders following the Silk Road, the vast network that connected Europe and Asia and provided a thoroughfare for the exchange and spread of not only products but also ideas.

The Soviets recognized the importance of the Karakum as a source of minerals in the second half of the 20th century and conducted archaeological and geographical studies to determine if it was suitable for other purposes.

The sand dunes of the Karakum Desert support only the hardiest of drought-resistant plant life.

DARVAZA GAS CRATER

In Derweze, a former village in the Karakum Desert, there is a hole in the ground that burns constantly. The Darvaza crater was first created in the 1950s when a Soviet oil rig that was drilling in the area collapsed into a pocket of natural gas below the soil. In 1971, Soviet engineers decided to burn off the methane gas to regain access to a drilling site—a process they thought would take several weeks. However, the gas never burned out, and the fire has continued ever since. The locals began calling the crater "Hell's Gate" or "The Door to Hell." The nation now sees the site as a tourist destination.

In 2004, the small village of Derweze was dismantled. The then-president of Turkmenistan, Saparmurat Niyazov, had traveled to the site of the crater and found the nearby village of approximately 350 people to be "an unpleasant site for tourists" and ordered its destruction.

A few visitors gaze at the flaming crater in the Karakum Desert.

Transportation and irrigation emerged as specific areas in need of further development.

In 1954, the USSR began construction of the world's largest irrigation canal. Since its completion in 1967, the Karakum Canal has watered the desert, running 520 miles (837 km) from the Amu Darya to Geok Tepe, a former fortress in the oasis of Ahal. Beginning in the 1970s, further construction extended the canal to the Caspian Sea, and today it is more than 870 miles (1,400 km) long. Nearly 300 miles (483 km) are navigable (wide and deep enough to be used by ships), though its main function is irrigation.

As engineers and geographers studied the desert for practical purposes, archaeologists conducted expeditions that resulted in important historical discoveries. Near the Geoksyur Oasis, scientists found that the canal was not

This aerial view shows a portion of the Karakum Canal, which irrigates the desert country.

For thousands of years, nomads in Central Asia have relied on the Arvana breed of dromedary camels for milk, wool, and transportation between their summer pastures and their winter homes. The camels are known, and specially bred, for their high yields of milk, a smooth ride, and the ability to carry heavy loads. They are raised across Turkmenistan, as well as in Uzbekistan, Azerbaijan, Kazakhstan, Turkey, northern Iran, and Afghanistan.

The Arvana is not the more familiar swift, long-legged beast found in the deserts of Saudi Arabia. Rather, it is a short, relatively slow animal, whose value lies in its ability to go without water and with little food for long periods of time. Also, it matures quickly. Females can bear two calves in three years, making it easier and more economical to increase their herd size.

A herd of Arvana dromedaries grazes in an oasis near Mary in Turkmenistan.

the first to be constructed in the desert. They unearthed, from deep beneath the sands, the remains of canals dating from 2000 to 3000 BCE. The dry desert sands had also preserved buildings, artifacts, and written documents from the same period near the capital, Ashgabat. Outside Dzheytun, archaeologists have discovered the remains of what many believe is the earliest agricultural settlement in west-central Asia.

Since World War II (1939—1945), the Karakum has become increasingly industrialized as factories and railroads have been built, oil and gas pipelines laid, and power stations erected. Where most people once lived as nomads, towns have grown up, fully supplied with electricity and gas. Irrigation has enabled the cultivation of cotton, fruit, and vegetable crops not only around the oases but also well beyond.

ASHGABAT

The capital city of Ashgabat, which is also the nation's largest city, lies in southern Turkmenistan near the Iranian border. The Karakum Canal runs through the city, which is home to around 846,000 people (as of 2020).

In ancient times, it was an important outpost along the Silk Road, where caravans stopped to unload and reload as their goods made their way across

Ashgabat gleams with an abundance of white marble buildings.

Central Asia. At Ashgabat, the routes divided, and caravans could continue their trip either along the northern leg, which wound through the mountains, or they could head south to an alternate road through the desert. The city survived under the name of Konjikala until the 13th century, when the Mongols destroyed it on their rampage through Central Asia. In the following centuries, it was a seasonal nomad camp until the Russians arrived in the 19th century. They built it up into a European-style city. In 1925, during the early Soviet era, the city was named as the capital of the Turkmen Soviet Socialist Republic; then in 1991, it became the capital of the independent nation of Turkmenistan.

In 1948, a powerful earthquake destroyed much of the city, which has since been rebuilt. As part of this reconstruction, President Saparmurat Niyazov undertook an extensive renovation project to build his vision of "the White City." He oversaw the construction of 543 spectacular white marble buildings, in addition to many monuments and golden statues of himself. In 2013, the city was included in the *Guinness World Records* as having the world's highest concentration of white marble buildings.

Today, the city is a sprawling, modern city in the middle of a desert, its white marble district said to be eerily grandiose and empty. In fact, it is jokingly (though quietly) called "the city of the dead." It also has huge, Soviet-style apartment blocks and traditional Turkmen brick houses, along with many bazaars, hotels, museums, mosques, and an Olympic sports complex. In 2019, Ashgabat was named the world's most expensive city for expatriate employees (not necessarily for residents) by ECA International's Cost of Living survey.

EARTHQUAKES

At the end of the 19th and beginning of the 20th centuries, Turkmenistan was repeatedly plagued by earthquakes—in 1893, 1895, 1924, and 1929. Then, in 1948, it was hit by one of the 10 deadliest earthquakes in recorded history.

In early October of 1948, an earthquake measuring 7.3 on the Richter scale struck Turkmenistan in the area around Ashgabat. The city was completely destroyed. At the time, Turkmenistan was part of the Soviet Union. As part of Soviet leader Joseph Stalin's policy of secrecy, accounts of the earthquake marginalized the scale of the damage and underreported the number of people killed. Although it was reported then that 10,000 people had died in the massive earthquake, the real number was probably closer to 110,000 or even higher—nearly 90 percent of the population of Ashgabat. Communist party functionaries closed the city to outsiders for more than a year. Nearly five years passed before all the bodies of the victims were recovered from the rubble and ruins.

Today, a monument and a museum, both in Ashgabat, have been dedicated to the victims of the tragedy, and October 6 is known as Remembrance Day and is observed as a national day of mourning in their honor. A cemetery in the northern part of the city holds the remains of the dead.

In 2000, another strong earthquake hit western Turkmenistan, measuring 7.0, with its epicenter in the sparsely populated mountains north of Balkanabad. Official sources in the country reported no deaths, but unofficially, there were said to be 11 casualties.

INTERNET LINKS

https://www.advantour.com/turkmenistan/nature.htm
This travel site provides information about the geographical features of Turkmenistan.

https://www.nationalgeographic.com/news/ energy/2014/07/140716-door-to-hell-darvaza-crater-george- kourounis-expedition/#close
This article describes one explorer's descent into the Darvaza crater.

https://www.theatlantic.com/photo/2013/06/the-city-of-white- marble-ashgabat-turkmenistan/100528
This photo essay features 20 intriguing pictures of Ashgabat.

HISTORY

The archaeological ruins of ancient Merv mark the site of what was once an important oasis city along the Silk Road.

2

THE HISTORY OF TURKMENISTAN IS very much the history of Central Asia. Prior to the 20th century, it's an account of an area and a people, but not of a nation. Until the 1920s, Turkmenistan had no established borders with neighboring regions, no central economy or government, and no distinct national identity. Ruled and contested by legendary empires led by Genghis Khan, Timur, and Alexander the Great, the area's long tradition of tribal governance and clan loyalties served its people well until the pervasive and often all-consuming rule of the Soviets was established.

The earliest history of the Turkmen people is not contained in written records or in oral accounts passed down through the generations. It is reflected in the archaeological remains that offer glimpses into the lives of the inhabitants of the earliest settlements and encampments. The climate of Central Asia may have made the region inhospitable to settlement, but its sand and relatively dry conditions have also preserved evidence of how and where people once lived. Scientific advances such as

The oasis city of Merv was an ancient urban center on the Murgab River. Dating from the Achaemenid era in the sixth century BCE, the city reached its peak in the 12th and 13th centuries, with a population of 500,000. In 1221, invading Mongol armies destroyed the city, reportedly killing everyone in it. Today, the Merv ruins are a protected World Heritage archaeological site.

This illustration, which is exhibited at the National History and Ethnology Museum in Mary, depicts a scene of Turkmen living in yurts.

carbon-14 dating have solved even more mysteries about the region's earliest and most successful initial settlers.

Scholars disagree about where the first people to settle in Central Asia, and in particular the area then known as Turkistan, came from. Nevertheless, they do agree that these first residents were probably nomadic goat herders. Occupying caves and portable structures called yurts, they left traces of their existence on cave walls and under shifting sands to be discovered centuries later. Around 6000 BCE, some of the region's inhabitants began to construct settlements out of simple mud bricks.

In parts of what is today Turkmenistan, ruins of palaces, public buildings, and irrigation canals testify to the existence of large urban areas dating back to the third millennium BCE. In the centuries that followed, conquests and increased trade contacts with the outside world changed life in these expanding urban centers. Generally, however, the culture seems to have altered little, continuing as it had for more than 5,000 years. Within this culture, three patterns of living emerged: nomadic, pastoralist, and settled.

EARLY NOMADS, PASTORALISTS, AND SETTLERS

Nomads maintained temporary settlements in more than one place. Their settlements were not unplanned, however. Based on how they fed, clothed, and housed themselves, they sought out and returned to the same locations year after year. Nomads fell into two categories. Hunters and gatherers made up the first group. Their movements were based on the need to find places for seasonal hunting and harvesting in areas where they could endure the extremes of the climate. Herders—breeders of domesticated animals—formed the second group. They moved primarily to find pastureland for their animals, on which they depended for food, shelter, and clothing.

Pastoralists lived in small villages where permanent houses provided shelter for individual families. The land surrounding the village was used to grow food for the villagers and their animals, but it was primarily used as pastureland. Though pastoralists did some farming, primarily raising grains, they relied mostly on their animals for their food and other needs, much as the herding nomads had done. Even though the pastoralists had permanent dwellings, they moved to the mountains in the summer, when the heat in the mud houses became unbearable and the animals did not have enough water. In the mountains, they lived in yurts that they dismantled and brought back with them to the lowlands until the next summer.

While nomads and pastoralists had at least two locations that could provide the subsistence-level economy they needed, people in the settlements had to make a living solely in one place. Most settlements were agriculturally based, which restricted their location and placement to the delta plains of the Amu Darya, Gorgan, and Atrek Rivers. There, villagers developed irrigation systems that enabled them to produce enough food for their own consumption as well as for trade with neighboring villages. One of the region's villages eventually became a bustling city where people developed crafts and services that they could trade with neighboring villages and migrating nomads for raw materials and animals.

Though the lands that lay to the east of the Caspian Sea could boast of 300 days of sunshine a year, the accompanying heat and drought never made the area attractive to conquerors as a permanent place to settle. Nevertheless, the region was important from ancient times as a route to more desirable and hospitable destinations. As such, it experienced the ravages and onslaughts of many invaders. Starting in 600 BCE, it was part of the vast Persian Empire until Alexander the Great passed through the region 250 years later on his way to India. The Greeks, who arrived next, built cities and towns that would prove to be of great importance to the trade routes that united China in the East and Europe in the West in the vast network known as the Silk Road. Three hundred years later, at Nisa, near today's Ashgabat, the Parthians established their capital as they tried to hold back the Roman quest for lands in the East.

The Parthian Fortresses of Nisa is a UNESCO World Heritage Site.

Since 1975, the United Nations Educational, Scientific and Cultural Organization (UNESCO) has maintained a list of international landmarks or regions considered to be of "outstanding value" to the people of the world. Such sites embody the common natural and cultural heritage of humanity, and therefore deserve particular protection. The organization

works with the host country to establish plans for managing and conserving their sites. UNESCO also reports on sites that are in imminent or potential danger of destruction and can offer emergency funds to try to save the property.

The organization is continually assessing new sites for inclusion on the World Heritage List. In order to be selected, a site must be of "outstanding universal value" and meet at least one of ten criteria. These required elements include cultural value—that is, artistic, religious, or historical significance—and natural value, including exceptional beauty, unusual natural phenomenon, and scientific importance. As of August 2020, there were 1,121 sites listed: 869 cultural, 213 natural, and 39 mixed (cultural and natural) properties in 167 nations. Of those, 53 are listed as "in danger."

Turkmenistan has three sites on the World Heritage List, all categorized as cultural. All three places are of importance in the country's pre-Soviet history. Kunya-Urgench in the northwest contains the archaeological ruins of monuments dating from the 11th to the 16th centuries that reflect the architectural design of several cultural periods. The Parthian Fortresses of Nisa is the site of one of the earliest and most important cities of the Parthian Empire, a major power from the mid-third century BCE to the third century CE. Finally, the State Historical and Cultural Park of "Ancient Merv" in the region of Mary, is perhaps the most significant World Heritage Site in Turkmenistan. Its ruins, including the fortress shown above, mark the oldest and best-preserved of the oasis-cities along the Silk Route in Central Asia, reflecting 4,000 years of history.

THE SILK ROAD

Few people traveled the full length of the Silk Road, more accurately called the Silk Roads, since many trade routes connecting China and India with Europe threaded their way across the deserts and through the mountains of Central Asia. Beginning from the East in the northern Chinese city of Xi'an, as many as 800 caravans towed by camels carried silk, satin, rubies, diamonds, pearls, musk, and rhubarb. Traded sometimes at 20-mile (32 km) intervals, these goods changed hands many times before they reached the West. Loaded with commodities such as medicines, gold, grapes, pomegranates, woolen rugs, colored glass, and green and white jade from the West, the caravan would then head back to its place of origin.

Traders traveled over, around, and through mountain ranges, skirting the deserts when they could and crossing them only if they had to. Towns grew up and thrived in the deserts around the more hospitable oases. The legendary city of Merv established itself as an important stop, and its ruins are found near the present-day city of Mary in Turkmenistan.

The ruins of ancient settlements in Turkmenistan include dozens of villages and several cities.

Rather than describe the Silk Road by geographical distance, traders found it more useful to describe it in terms of travel time: By camel, the Silk Road was a six-month journey from east to west and a trip of one month or more from north to south. Distances calculated by time allowed travelers to plan how far they would have to go not just to reach their destination but also to replenish their food and water supplies and to find shelter. Often traders would be forced to travel for several weeks, taking with them everything they personally needed during that time in addition to the items they wished to trade. They had to plan their travels for times when they could expect to survive with no more shelter than the simple structures they could carry.

Besides material goods, travelers conveyed their art, food, music, and lifestyles along the Silk Road. Today, centuries later, foods, artistic designs, and musical instruments that resemble each other appear in towns and villages spread thousands of miles apart thanks to the shared cultural experience of the Silk Road.

THE ARRIVAL OF ISLAM

In the eighth century, Arab Islamic armies first conquered the land that would become Turkmenistan. Though conquests and invasions had been occurring in the region's deserts and mountains for more than 1,200 years, they ultimately influenced the conquerors more than the Turkmen. Throughout those centuries, the native residents had continued to live as they always had, as nomads or pastoralists, raising and moving their animals and maintaining their cultural and religious traditions. However, the introduction of Islam and its religious and political domination had an enormous impact on the region's inhabitants, most of whom remain Muslim to this day.

By the 11th century, tribes of Turkmen had begun to migrate west from their mountain homes to settle, at least for part of the year, near the Caspian Sea. At that time, this area was ruled by the Turks. Subsequently, under the leadership of Genghis Khan, the Mongols conquered the Turks in the 13th century. For the next 200 years, the Mongols ruled the land until they, too, were expelled, this time by an Uzbek invasion of the area. Until the mid-19th century, this area, known then as Turkmenia, was ruled by two khanates, or Islamic kingdoms, Khiva and Bukhara. In 1873, Russia incorporated the khanate of Khiva into its empire to improve its own access to the trade routes of Central Asia.

RUSSIAN RULE

In the 19th century, a new superpower emerged to the north of Central Asia—the Russian Empire. The Russian czars and their administrations made clear their interest in developing trade relations with Central Asian khanates as well as in ending slave trade in the region. In addition, czarist military ministers were interested in establishing military and diplomatic control of the area, as they became increasingly alarmed by the aggressive British takeover of the Indian subcontinent, Afghanistan, and Persia. During that time, very little was known in Russia and Europe about the khanates. Their cultures remained a mystery, and their supposed wealth became the focal point of numerous legends. Tales of diamonds, rubies, and hoards of gold hidden in palaces and the ruins of ancient cities were repeated again and again.

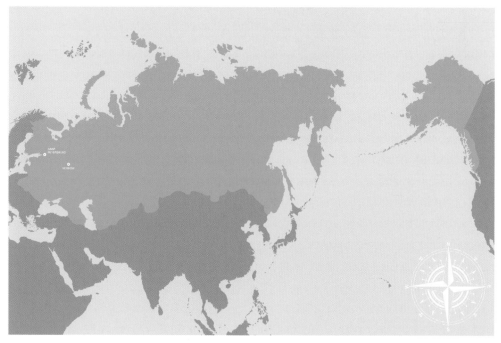

The gold portion of this map shows the extent of the Russian Empire in the 19th century.

Throughout the centuries, the Turkmen had remained nomads, loyal to none and enemy to almost everyone. Their reputation as kidnappers and outlaws ensured that no one took seriously their claims to their lands and caused those who had been victimized by their banditry to support the Russian invaders.

Turkmen resistance to the encroachment of the Russians was the strongest of any that was mobilized in Central Asia. However, by the end of the 19th century, the Russian Empire was firmly established. In 1869, a port on the Caspian Sea, known today as Turkmenbashi (or Türkmenbasy), was founded. From there, Russian soldiers conducted raids against Turkmen settlements, slaughtering people and destroying their property and animals. The definitive defeat of the Turkmen tribes came in 1881, when the Russians captured their last stronghold, Geok Tepe, northwest of Ashgabat.

More than 7,000 Turkmen died in the battle for the city, and another 8,000 were massacred as they fled into the desert. Today, the battle is marked by a national day of mourning each year, and the resistance the Turkmen mounted is often cited as a source of great national pride. The Russians continued their attacks by moving on to Merv and Ashgabat, following the orders of a general whose motto was: "The harder you hit them, the longer they'll stay down." The approach proved effective, and by 1894, all the land reaching to the Caspian Sea belonged to the czar. In 1897, agreements with Afghanistan and Persia established the borders with these countries, and the Russian annexation of Turkmenistan was complete.

Throughout this period, today's Turkmenistan was often ruled by corrupt military officers and Russian administrators. Cities began to grow as Russians moved into the area, and the railroads linked them to cities in other Russian colonies. Nomads, in particular, found their lifestyle difficult to sustain as Russian settlers poured into the countryside, seizing pastureland and converting it into farmland for the cultivation of crops.

THE BOLSHEVIKS AND THE SOVIET SYSTEM

In 1917, there was a long and bloody revolution in Russia. It began with an insurrection of workers and soldiers that overthrew the czar and seized control of the government. The Bolsheviks, a Russian socialist political group,

The Turkmen collective farmers shown here were paid part of their yearly income in a Soviet farm administration office sometime between 1930 and 1940.

were locked in a bitter civil war against loyalist forces for nearly five years. During this period, many parts of Central Asia regained a significant degree of autonomy, or self-rule, from the Russian authorities. Only in 1921 and 1922 did the Bolsheviks re-establish their control over most of Central Asia.

In 1922, the Bolsheviks established the communist Union of Soviet Socialist Republics (USSR), or the Soviet Union, in place of what had been the Russian Empire. Turkmenistan became the Turkmen Soviet Socialist Republic. The Soviets launched plans to reform all of Central Asia. In the 1930s, Joseph Stalin implemented a radical new policy throughout the republic as he forced Turkmen onto large collective, or group, farms, seizing their pastureland and destroying their herds. Throughout Central Asia, famine became as familiar as the nomadic lifestyle had once been. Turkmen fled to Iran and Afghanistan or into the Karakum Desert. By 1936, in their effort to preserve their nomadic

DEFINING COMMUNISM

Communism is a political, social, and economic philosophy in which all property is publicly owned and each person works and is paid (by the government) according to their abilities and needs, as determined by the government. This doctrine is the opposite of liberal democracy and capitalism. Theoretically, a communist society is a classless system and was conceived as a way of eliminating the wide disparity between the rich and the poor, which in czarist Russia was enormous, and to eliminate the exploitation of workers.

The communist economy is based on central planning, the opposite of free-market capitalism. In a centrally planned economic system, a central authority, such as the government, makes all decisions regarding the manufacturing and distribution of products. It determines prices and wages. In market economies, those decisions are traditionally made by businesses and consumers. Historically, most centrally planned economies are based on communism and are characteristic of authoritarian rule.

In independent Turkmenistan, communism is no longer the political or economic system. However, it is stilled largely centrally planned, in that the president and his authorities exercise total control over the economy, and private ownership is completely secondary to government supervision.

way of life, more than a million Turkmen had become refugees in the desert or in neighboring countries. Many of their descendants remain there today.

Throughout this time, Turkmenistan was ruled from Moscow. However, its remote and far-flung communities were less affected than the more urbanized Russia by Moscow's cultural policies. Still, the Soviet cultural machine reduced the influence of family and tribal loyalties, redefining them as old-fashioned and unprogressive. Russians were installed in all important government offices, and Russian became Turkmenistan's official language. Religious practices were also discouraged to the point of nearly disappearing.

Only in the mid-1980s did the situation begin to change, as the liberal-minded Soviet leader Mikhail Gorbachev came to power and launched a program of greater freedom and openness called perestroika. By the late 1980s, democratic reform movements swept through many of the satellite republics and the whole of the Soviet Union itself. However, their effects stopped short

Statues of Turkmen heroes surround a golden statue of President Saparmurat Niyazov (*center*) in front of the Independence Monument in Ashgabat.

of Turkmenistan, where the entrenched Communist Party survived without change until it became the ruling party of the newly independent Turkmenistan in 1991. The only significant change was its new name, the Democratic Party of Turkmenistan.

INDEPENDENCE

Independent Turkmenistan's first ruler was Saparmurat Niyazov, whose totalitarian rule predated the changes of 1991. His domination of the government and the Turkmen people violated the laws and constitution of the country. Under his leadership, Turkmenistan pursued a course of internal repression and international isolation, and in 1999, the Turkmenistani government declared Niyazov president for life. That reign came to an end when he died in December 2006.

Gurbanguly Berdimuhamedov, a dentist before he entered government, had served under Niyazov as the minister of health and then, beginning in 2001, as vice president. He became the country's new president and won Turkmenistan's first multi-candidate presidential election in February 2007, and again in 2012 and 2017 with over 97 percent of the vote in both instances. Outside observers viewed both elections as undemocratic. Like his predecessor, Berdimuhamedov rules with absolute authority in a cult of personality. He is portrayed as a heroic, larger-than-life idol to be worshipped and adored without question. This portrayal is supported by government-controlled mass media, propaganda, enormous portraits and statues, and grand spectacles of patriotism. Typically, this sort of leader holds absolute power in totalitarian or authoritarian countries.

Turkmenistan's president Gurbanguly Berdimuhamedov holds up his credentials during his inauguration ceremony on February 14, 2017.

As president, Saparmurat Niyazov took the name Turkmenbashi, which means "Father of all Turkmen." He lectured young people on their appearance, telling them to give up the long hair, beards, and multiple gold teeth that had become fashionable. He banned smoking in public places as a result of his own experience with heart disease. Many of his followers called him the "national prophet." Indeed, Turkmenbashi basked in a deified public glow during his reign.

Niyazov wrote a book called Ruhnama, or Book of the Soul, which is a mishmash of autobiography peppered with poetry; a glorified history of the Turkmen people; and a guide to spiritual, moral living for Turkmenistanis. The book became required reading in schools, universities, and governmental organizations. Notably, questions based on the book's content were even included on the national driver's test, as the president evidently believed his moral principles would guide his people to drive safely, with consideration for others. In March 2006, shortly before he died, Niyazov announced that he had arranged with Allah (the Muslim name for God) that anyone who read Ruhnama three times would automatically go to heaven.

In an effort to reshape Turkmen culture to his own likeness, Niyazov changed the days of the week, months of the year, and many place names to those honoring his own family—naming April for his mother, for example. He channeled an enormous amount of the country's wealth from oil, natural gas, and other resources into vanity projects, such as an ice palace in the desert and gold statues of himself (such as the one shown above, at the Independence Monument in Ashgabat). A 39-foot (12 m) tall gold-plated figure of Niyazov once stood atop a colossal monument called the Neutrality Arch, where it rotated, always facing the sun.

Niyazov's hubris could have been written off as mere quirkiness, but there was a very dark side to his rule. He was considered by many international human rights activists and organizations to be one of the most brutal, totalitarian dictators in the *world. Government torture of dissidents was common—and people could be considered dissidents simply by being seen reading a foreign newspaper or listening to forbidden broadcasts. Freedom of expression and opposition of any sort were not tolerated. To express dissatisfaction with the president or his government was considered treason. Under Turkmenbashi's iron fist, the living standards of his citizens deteriorated sharply.*

In 2002, Niyazov was the target of an assassination attempt. As part of the investigation and the purges it subsequently triggered, more than 1,000 people were arrested and convicted in trials that were either conducted in secret or for public display. Some observers alleged that the coup attempt was arranged by Niyazov himself, to provide him with a reason to further cement his power.

The president was known to have a cardiac condition, and on December 21, 2006, the state media announced that Niyazov had died at age 66 of heart failure.

INTERNET LINKS

https://www.bbc.com/news/world-asia-16098048
This timeline provides a chronology of key events in the history of Turkmenistan.

https://www.newyorker.com/magazine/2007/05/28/the-golden-man
This lengthy article by travel writer Paul Theroux chronicles his visit to Turkmenistan during the time of Saparmurat Niyazov's rule.

https://www.thoughtco.com/turkmenistan-facts-and-history-195771
A quick synopsis of Turkmenistan's pre-Soviet history is provided on this site.

http://whc.unesco.org/en/statesparties/TM
This is the World Heritage page for sites in Turkmenistan.

GOVERNMENT

The green and red flags of Turkmenistan wave on a windy day in Ashgabat.

3

TECHNICALLY, TURKMENISTAN IS A multi-party presidential republic based on a constitution. The president is both the head of state and the head of government; the branches of government—executive, legislative, and judicial—operate independently, providing a balance of power. This is what is stated in the constitution. In reality, however, Turkmenistan is an authoritarian dictatorship and has been from its earliest years of independence.

POLITICAL HISTORY

The political climate in Turkmenistan has been shaped by two powerful historical influences—the traditional tribal social structure and the communist system of government that established Turkmenistan as a Soviet republic in the early 20th century.

Until the Soviet Union created the Turkmen Soviet Socialist Republic, the people living there, like the people throughout Central Asia, lived as either nomadic or settled. These divisions were not national or ethnic and certainly not political. Nomads and settled people had lifestyles that

The flag of Turkmenistan has a bright green background with a vertical red stripe on the left side. In the stripe are five guls, complex medallion designs used in the country's woven carpets, which represent the five main Turkmen tribes. Below them, olive branches symbolize neutrality. Against the green, there are five white stars, representing the five administrative regions, and a crescent moon, the symbol of Islam.

best suited their individual and preferred methods of earning a living. Within these two broad divisions, people belonged to tribes and clans.

The Soviet method of running a country clashed with this existing structure. The Soviet approach was to assign people to collective units in the hope of breaking down family and ethnic ties and replacing those loyalties with allegiance to the Soviet state. The strength of tribal bonds in Soviet Turkmenistan, however, proved particularly resistant to change and resettlement. The central administrators in Moscow found that collective farms formed according to tribal division were the best possible compromise. One result of this slight deviation in standard practice was that people in the countryside never lost their strong ties to their tribes, and their traditions and loyalties were easily reestablished after the fall of the Soviet empire.

When the Soviet Union disintegrated in 1991, the Soviet Central Asian republics declared their independence from the government in Moscow. Though Turkmenistan was a nation that had just been given its freedom, it asserted its independence less enthusiastically than the others. Its ruling party took as its name the Democratic Party of Turkmenistan (DPT) and officially broke away from the Soviet Communist Party. However, of the Democratic Party's 52,000 members, around 48,000 were former Communists. In addition, all the executive and legislative leaders of the pre-independence period remained in office. Of particular significance to Turkmenistan's future was the leadership of Saparmurat Niyazov, who had been the leader under the Soviets and continued as such—becoming "president for life" in 1999—in independent Turkmenistan.

If democracy simply means that people are granted the opportunity to vote for their leaders, Turkmenistan is a democracy. In the 1992 election, Niyazov ran unopposed and won the vote. In the 2017 presidential election—the most recent as of 2020—97.7 percent of the vote went to the incumbent president Gurbanguly Berdimuhamedov, who was essentially unopposed as well.

However, if democracy means that people are allowed to form their own parties and be elected in opposition to the party in power, Turkmenistan is definitely not a democracy. Opposition is not allowed, and although there are three political parties (as of 2020), all three support the president.

THE CONSTITUTION

National constitutions can be beautiful things. These official documents lay the legal foundation upon which a government and society will function. They typically describe a system that reveres human rights, freedoms, and justice within the construct of a country's particular culture. The texts inevitably declare the source of the government's power to be grounded in the people—for example, Turkmenistan's Article 3 states, "Sovereignty is exercised by the people of Turkmenistan, the people are the sole source of the state power"—and go on to lay out a foundation of ideals. However, the extent to which any nation's political reality reflects the constitutional ideal is a matter of how vigorously those ideals are enforced. Most nations naturally have some gap between the ideal and the actual, but in Turkmenistan's case, it's quite a wide one.

During Niyazov's regime, only one political party was allowed, the ruling Democratic Party of Turkmenistan (DPT). When Berdimuhamedov became president, the constitution was amended to allow for multiple political parties, but any true opposition was immediately squashed, and the existing parties are loyal to the DPT.

The country's constitution of 2016 sounds very good on paper. It emphasizes one of the country's most basic doctrines—its status of permanent neutrality. It also establishes the nation as a secular state that ensures the rights of its citizens. The constitution guarantees religious freedom, freedom of expression, the rule of law, and the right of peaceful assembly. In practice, few rights can be taken for granted in Turkmenistan.

THE EXECUTIVE BRANCH

The president is elected for a term of seven years. He (as yet there has not been a woman president) works with the National Assembly (the legislative body) to implement laws, oversees the armed forces, establishes foreign policy, and appoints various ministers and judges. In addition, "the President of Turkmenistan shall issue decrees, regulations and orders, binding on the entire territory of Turkmenistan" (Article 72 of the constitution) and has "the right to immunity. His honour and dignity shall be protected by law" (Article 74).

THE LEGISLATIVE BRANCH

Prior to 2008, the legislature was bicameral, that is, it had two houses. One was the Khalk Maslahaty, or People's Council, a body of around 2,500 delegates—some elected and others appointed. The other was the National Assembly, or Mejilis. After the constitution was revised in 2008, the People's Council was demoted, so to speak, and reorganized as the Council of Elders, a strictly advisory group. Meanwhile, the number of seats in the Mejilis was increased to 125. Members are directly elected to five-year terms from single-seat constituencies by an absolute majority vote. Following the 2018 elections, the Mejilis was comprised of 94 men and 31 women. The next election was set for 2023. For a time, the Mejilis was the sole legislative house in the parliament.

However, in 2017, President Berdimuhamedov issued a decree transforming the Council of Elders back into the People's Council, effective following the

The Oguzhan Presidential Palace is part of a complex of government buildings in Ashgabat.

Following the death of Niyazov in 2006, Gurbanguly Berdimuhamedov became the nation's second president. Although he took some measures to reverse some of Niyazov's quirkier policies—for example, the banning of operas and circuses as being "insufficiently Turkmen"—he quickly established himself as an authoritarian strongman like his predecessor. In 2016, he changed the constitution to remove term limits, effectively allowing him to rule for life. Before that, he won elections that were internationally condemned as fraudulent.

Berdimuhamedov has built his own cult of personality based on his own flamboyant eccentricities—he often poses with fancy sports cars, holding puppies, riding elegant horses, or performing feats of

strength or daring. He dubbed himself "Father Protector" and erected his own massive statues of gold in his likeness.

In 2010, Berdimuhamedov had former president Niyazov's Neutrality Arch dismantled and moved from Ashgabat to an outlying town. In its new location, the golden statue of Niyazov no longer rotates with the sun. Meanwhile, in 2015, a 69-foot (21 m) gold leaf statue of Berdimuhamedov on horseback atop an enormous block of white marble (above) was unveiled in Ashgabat.

In 2019, the organization Human Rights Watch reported Turkmenistan to be "one of the world's most closed and repressively governed countries." This shows that things have not changed much in Turkmenistan between the reign of its two presidents.

2018 regional and local elections. As of 2020, the status and function of the revamped legislature was still being determined.

THE JUDICIAL BRANCH

The Supreme Court consists of the court president and 21 associate judges, all appointed by the president for five-year terms. The president can also dismiss judges at will. The court is organized into civil, criminal, and military chambers. The Supreme Court only hears cases of national importance; it does not hear appeals from lower court cases. Separate courts of appeal exist at the provincial level.

Although the constitution asserts the independence of the judiciary, in practice, the judges are wholly beholden to the president for their jobs. Therefore, their decisions almost certainly align with the president's will, and if not, the executive can modify those court decisions. Not surprisingly, therefore, corruption is said to be endemic in the courts.

In 2019, Transparency International ranked Turkmenistan at number 165 out of 180 countries in its Corruption Perceptions Index, which ranks countries by their perceived levels of public sector corruption. The lower the ranking, the lower the people's faith in the honesty and transparency of their government. Turkmenistan's ranking that year reflected a downward trend.

REGIONAL GOVERNMENT

Five administrative regions are served by the central government: Ahal, Balkan, Dashoguz, Lebap, and Mary—in which 20 cities and 46 towns are located. Each region is divided into a number of districts, which are administered by officials who are either appointed by the national government or elected with its approval.

ELECTIONS

The government of Turkmenistan strongly encourages all people over the age of 18 to vote, as much to show support for the system as to choose representatives, who must first be approved by the government before they can run for office. Despite such incentives as free towels and candy at the polls, it is not unusual for people to decline to vote. When the government finds that voter turnout is too low, poll workers carry the ballot boxes from house to house. Additionally, people unable to go to the polls can choose a representative to vote in their place. This practice can result in artificially high voter turnout figures. In the event that no one person achieves a majority, which can happen when there are multiple candidates running for the same office, a runoff election between the top candidates determines the winner.

A woman casts her ballot in Ashgabat during the parliamentary elections in March 2018.

INTERNET LINKS

https://www.businessinsider.com/turkmenistan-leader-gurbanguly-berdymukhamedov-biography-2020-1
This photo essay shines a light on President Gurbanguly Berdimuhamedov.

https://constituteproject.org/constitution/Turkmenistan_2016.pdf?lang=en
This site provides a pdf of Turkmenistan's most recent constitution, in English.

https://freedomhouse.org/country/turkmenistan/freedom-world/2020
Freedom House ranks each country annually in the Freedom in the World Index. (This link can be updated by year.)

https://www.hrw.org/sitesearch?search=Turkmenistan
This is the Human Rights Watch page for articles about Turkmenistan.

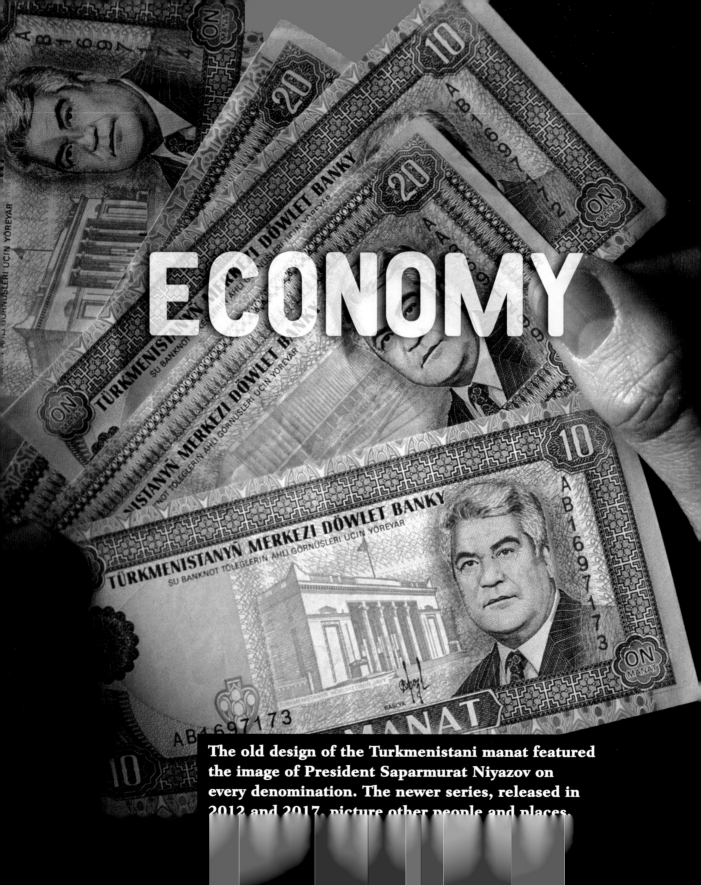

ECONOMY

The old design of the Turkmenistani manat featured the image of President Saparmurat Niyazov on every denomination. The newer series, released in 2012 and 2017, picture other people and places.

4

TURKMENISTAN'S ECONOMY IS based mainly on agriculture and the nation's significant natural gas and oil resources. Because the country is largely desert, crops are intensively grown in irrigated oases. The two primary crops are cotton—most of which is produced for export—and wheat, which is domestically consumed.

The country's mineral resources, meanwhile, brought in tremendous wealth in the mid-2000s, but little of that reached the average citizen. (The people did enjoy free or greatly subsidized utilities, such as natural gas and electricity, however.) More recently, lower energy prices have reduced government revenues. Nevertheless, the government continues to report economic growth. However, as with other state statistics, reliable economic data is not easily obtained from Turkmenistan's murky government sources.

Turkmenistan's industries are related to its mineral and agricultural products and include meat and fish processing, petroleum production, oil refining, the making of textiles, and the quarrying of building materials.

In 2020, Turkmenistan ranked 170 out of 180 countries on the Heritage Foundation's Index of Economic Freedom. The index ranks nations according to scores on 12 economic indicators, such as business and trade freedom, property rights, tax burden, governmental integrity, and fiscal health. It reports, "The economy of Turkmenistan remains one of the most repressed in the Index."

MINERAL RESOURCES

Turkmenistan is rich in mineral resources. Large oil and natural gas deposits lie along the coast of the Caspian Sea. Those gas reserves are estimated to be the world's fifth largest, after Russia, Iran, Qatar, and Saudi Arabia. These fossil fuel resources provide the country with 100 percent of its energy needs. It therefore has no nuclear industry, nor does it derive power from renewable sources. It also exports crude oil, refined petroleum products, and natural gas.

Whereas Russia was once the major importer of this natural gas, today most of it flows to China. The government is, however, interested in bringing its gas to new markets and has looked into building new pipelines for that purpose. A trans-Caspian pipeline would carry gas to Europe, while a line through Afghanistan and Pakistan to India would open up southern markets.

However, major financing, political, and security hurdles stand in the way and are unlikely to be solved anytime soon.

Officials are also working to develop the nation's other mineral resources, which include coal, sulfur, salt, phosphate, iodine, and lignite. In addition, Turkmenistan's gypsum and limestone have proved plentiful sources of building materials, for both domestic demand and export.

A vineyard grows outside of Ashgabat.

AGRICULTURE

Agriculture in Turkmenistan contributes 7.5 percent to the country's gross domestic product (GDP) and employs about 48.2 percent of the workforce. Only 4 percent of the total land area is cultivated; however, more of the land is able to be used for pasture. More than 90 percent of the land under cultivation is irrigated, which enables the cultivation of cotton and wheat, as mentioned, but also barley, sesame, millet, corn, melons, grapes for wine, and alfalfa.

In the Soviet era, farming was organized into government-owned, large-scale collective farms and small subsistence household plots for personal use. After independence, former collective farms were reorganized into "peasant associations," in which individuals lease and work the land. Each parcel is about 10 acres (4 hectares) in size. In addition, somewhat larger, private "dayhan (or dekhan) farms" were also created. These are typically about 40 acres (16 ha) big, and though they are considered private property, all land in the country is controlled by the government. Although the constitution allows for private land ownership, the concept is very limited: Land is non-transferable; it may not be sold, given as a gift, passed on through inheritance, or exchanged. The land is given by the state, but if a farmer fails to meet government standards, his or her "private ownership" can be revoked.

COTTON Cotton is Turkmenistan's leading crop. In 2019, the country was the world's ninth-largest producer and the seventh-largest exporter

A pile of cotton sits on the edge of a cotton field near the city of Mary in eastern Turkmenistan.

of cotton. In the arid environment of much of Turkmenistan's agricultural land, a crop like cotton requires irrigation.

The production of cotton in Turkmenistan was initiated by the Soviets. The Soviet planners saw the sparsely populated country of Turkmenistan as the cotton bowl for its textile industry, and with good reason, since the republic alone supplied most of the cotton used in the massive Soviet Union. Indeed, as a Soviet republic, Turkmenistan's contribution to the Soviet economic system was far greater than any support it received.

Today, cotton continues to dominate the agricultural sector, but poor irrigation and management practices have reportedly had a detrimental effect on quality and quantity. In addition, the government's use of forced labor and child labor in cotton fields has led consumer and human rights groups to call for corporate boycotts of the nation's cotton. (Many international human rights organizations consider Turkmenistan's enforced cotton-harvesting labor to be a form of slavery.) Around 90 global brands pledged not to use cotton from Turkmenistan in their products. In 2018, the U.S. government banned Turkmenistani cotton and textiles.

A cotton picker poses for the camera in Dashoguz in northern Turkmenistan.

Each September, the government requires tens of thousands of citizens to step away from their usual jobs to pick cotton. Quotas are set, and public sector employees—including teachers, doctors, nurses, and government office workers—are forced to meet them. The harvest often takes months to complete, and laborers work in alternating shifts. Some people are able to avoid the grueling manual labor by paying a bribe or hiring someone to replace them. (For example, a teacher wishing to avoid service would have to pay someone about $10.50 per month to work in their place; when on average a teacher makes about $87 per month in salary.) Businesses are required to contribute

Domesticated animals are a source of labor and products for Turkmenistan, with cattle and sheep supplying much of the region's meat, and horses and camels serving as work animals. Karakul sheep and silkworms are raised for the wool and silk they provide for Turkmenistan's rug weavers.

The Karakul sheep may well be the world's oldest domesticated breed. Carvings of the Karakul have been found on ancient Babylonian temples dating back to 1400 BCE. Their skins were highly prized by traders on the Silk Road. The Karakul is native to Central Asia, where it has thrived in the dry desert at high altitudes. Over the centuries, the harsh conditions of its home environment have bred exceptional hardiness into the breed. Its sharp teeth last long into old age, enabling it to forage in the scarce vegetation of the mountain deserts. Able to survive in the extreme heat and cold, Karakul sheep also possess a strong flocking instinct, and the mothers are attentive to their lambs. Both these traits are advantageous to the sheep as they travel long distances twice each year.

The Karakul sheep is called a fat-tailed sheep—a distinction that is more than just cosmetic—because its tail stores fat. The fat provides nourishment, much as the camel's hump does, in the marginal land where few other animals can survive.

One ewe can have as many as three lambs each year. The lambs are born with a curly, glossy black coat. The adult coat contains both long, silky fibers and a coarser layer of guard hairs that can be used in both woven and felt materials. Adult Karakuls can be brown, gray, and sometimes even white.

The silky fur of Karakul lambs is especially valued, but the wool, meat, milk, and fat of the adult sheep are equally precious to the thrifty nomadic Turkmen, who for centuries have moved their households to take the sheep to fresh pasturelands. The sheep have provided homes, tools, furnishings, and clothes as well as food for the people.

to this national undertaking with labor or money. This annual effort leaves institutions understaffed, which undermines other sectors of the economy.

A golden statue of Turkmenistani president Gurbanguly Berdimuhamedov adorns the entrance to the library building in Mary, which opened in 2011.

TOURISM

Turkmenistan is far from a bustling tourist destination. Relatively few people travel there for vacation or leisure activities—or indeed for any purpose whatsoever. In 2016, just 6,000 foreigners visited the country, including those who were part of official delegations. Reliable statistics are not available in any event, though the government keeps close track of the comings and goings of every traveler.

On the one hand, the government seeks to encourage tourism in Turkmenistan. It promotes its famous carpets, ancient archaeological sites, fabulous Akhal-Teke horses, lively music and dance traditions, and growing

Gross domestic product (GDP) is a measure of a country's total production. The number reflects the total value of goods and services produced over one year. Economists use it to determine whether a country's economy is growing or contracting. Growth is good, while a falling GDP means trouble. Dividing the GDP by the number of people in the country determines the GDP per capita (per person). This number provides an indication of a country's average standard of living—the higher the better.

In 2017, the GDP per capita (adjusted to purchasing power parity) in Turkmenistan was reportedly $18,200. That figure is considered average, and it ranked Turkmenistan at 97th out of 228 countries listed by the CIA World Factbook. For comparison, the United States that year was number 19, with a GDP per capita of $59,500. Turkmenistan's neighbors ranked much lower to somewhat higher. Tajikistan was 192nd with a GDP per capita of $3,200, and Kyrgyzstan was 183rd with a GDP per capita of $3,700. Uzbekistan ranked 158th, with a GDP per capita of $6,900, and Kazakhstan ranked the highest of the Central Asian nations at 79th, with a GDP per capita of $26,300.

Tourists visit a mosque in the ancient city of Merv.

number of hotels. At international trade shows, the products and performing arts that make Turkmenistan attractive are on open display, and visitors are drawn to the possibility of travel there.

However, the nation's strict authoritarianism is off-putting to many travelers. For one thing, potential visitors must apply for a visa, which is not readily granted. Also, the government requires visitors wishing to explore the country (beyond the city limits) to have an assigned guide. Special additional permits are required to visit certain places.

The official state tourism website, tourism.gov.tm, promotes the country's highlights and also offers this curious adage: "Travel makes you modest in two ways: 1. You see what a tiny place you occupy in the world. 2. Makes you discover that everyone is wrong about other countries."

Turkmenistan is accessible by air though its impressive new airport outside of Ashgabat, which opened in 2017. Architecturally, the beautiful main terminal resembles a Turkmen falcon, and it features an abundance of dazzling white marble. Although the Ashgabat International Airport was designed to serve up to 14 million passengers a year, it's reported to be "eerily empty."

INTERNET LINKS

https://www.antislavery.org/wp-content/uploads/2019/04/Turkmenistan-Turkey-report.pdf
This human rights report examines the use of enforced labor in Turkmenistan's cotton industry.

https://en.turkmen.news/news/cotton-harvest-2019-review-disastrous-in-parts-of-turkmenistan
Turkmen.news, an independent news and human rights organization based in the Netherlands, reports on the cotton harvest situation.

https://www.heritage.org/index/country/turkmenistan
This site provides Turkmenistan's rating on the Index of Economic Freedom and an overview of its economy.

http://tourism.gov.tm
The nation's state tourism site in somewhat broken English offers an interesting presentation.

https://www.worldatlas.com/articles/the-biggest-industries-in-turkmenistan.html
This article provides an overview of industry in Turkmenistan.

ENVIRONMENT

Rippled sand dunes make up part of the landscape of the Repetek Biosphere State Reserve in the Karakum Desert.

5

LIKE ALL FORMER SOVIET REPUBLICS, Turkmenistan reaped the consequences of many decades of Moscow's environmental disregard and mismanagement. The leaders of present-day Turkmenistan also don't give top priority to environmental health.

The country's comparatively low levels of heavy industry and motor vehicle use have spared it from some of the air pollution problems that afflict more developed nations. However, it does grapple with soil and groundwater contamination caused by pesticides, fertilizers, and other agricultural chemicals. In addition, widespread use of irrigation has caused environmental damage of irreparable extent. Turkmenistan's diversion of Amu Darya waters into irrigation has directly led to the drying up of the Aral Sea. That, in turn, has resulted in increased desertification, soil salinization, and erosion. The Karakum and Kyzylkum Deserts grow by hundreds of thousands of acres annually.

Turkmenistan has 9 nature reserves and 13 sanctuaries, covering a total of about 4 percent of the nation's territory. The most recent, the Bereketli Garagum Nature Reserve, was designated in 2013. It covers 215,000 acres (87,000 ha) of the Karakum Desert in Ahal Province.

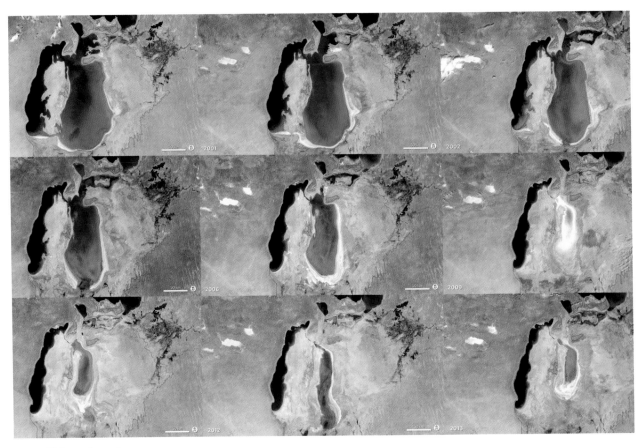

A SHRINKING LAKE

The Aral Sea is, or was, located north of Turkmenistan, between Uzbekistan and eastern Kazakhstan. In 1950, the Aral Sea was the fourth-largest lake in the world, surpassed in size only by the Caspian Sea, Lake Victoria, and Lake Superior. Today, what little remains of the sea is in danger of disappearing altogether.

Short-sighted Soviet planning in the mid-20th century drained the rivers for years to irrigate desert cotton fields, including those in Turkmenistan. Cotton requires a tremendous amount of water. As a result, the lake dried up, and the region suffered great contamination. The loss of water led to the disappearance of wildlife that the lake supported.

Fourteen cubic miles (60 cubic km) of water once drained into the Aral Sea from the Amu Darya and Syr Darya rivers. (The Amu Darya runs through

much of Turkmenistan before reaching the Aral Sea region.) After the Soviets had turned Central Asia into their own private cotton basin, diverting and draining the rivers in the process, the Aral Sea received so little water that it was only one-tenth of its former size and no longer one contiguous body of water. By 2018, it was largely gone.

The Karakum Canal carries water from the Amu Darya to irrigate crops in Turkmenistan.

However, it was not quite gone. The North Aral Sea remains and has been somewhat revived by restoration efforts in Kazakhstan, which built a dam and a canal for this purpose. The South Aral Sea, however, has been left to its fate, as Uzbekistan, Turkmenistan, and other Aral Sea basin countries continue to divert Amu Darya river waters for cotton irrigation. The dried up seabed of the South Aral Sea is now desert land with a high salt content. Dust storms regularly blow this salty soil to northwest Turkmenistan.

In addition, the Soviet biological-weapons research station—where scientists experimented with and disposed of viruses and bacteria in the hopes of developing biological weapons—now lies abandoned on what was once

Turkmenistan reveres its "golden horses," a distinctive, ancient Turkmen breed called Akhal-Teke. The horse is featured on the nation's official coat of arms as well as on its banknotes and postage stamps. Monuments to the horse are prominent in Ashgabat and other Turkmenistani cities. President Gurbanguly Berdimuhamedov is passionate about the breed and is often pictured astride one. In fact, a 69-foot (21 m) gold leaf statue of Berdimuhamedov on horseback tops an enormous block of white marble in Ashgabat. In 1970, long before he became president, he wrote a book called Akhalteke, Our Pride and Glory. *More recently, the leader broadcast a video of him singing a self-penned song to one of his horses—he is thought to have hundreds of them.*

President Gurbanguly Berdimuhamedov poses with an Akhal-Teke horse at a horse beauty contest in Ashgabat in 2016.

The horses are famous for their golden-brown coats—though some have coats of other colors—which have a somewhat metallic sheen. They have a reputation for their speed, endurance, and intelligence.

The Russian takeover of Turkmenistan in the late 19th century proved a threat to the breed's continued existence. For many years, authorities undertook to crossbreed the horses, hoping to produce a better animal, but the project was ultimately unsuccessful. During the Soviet era, private ownership of horses was outlawed, and the population of Akhal-Tekes went into steep decline.

Today, enthusiasts like Berdimuhamedov have reversed that decline, but there still remain less than 7,000 Akhal-Tekes in the world.

Vozrozhdeniya Island in the Aral Sea. As the sea shrank, Vozrozhdeniya lost its status as an island, first becoming a peninsula and then simply a part of the land. Though the Soviets had promised to clean up the area, their efforts were insufficient, and live anthrax spores—a deadly bacteria—were still present. In 2002, the United States sent a team of workers to clean up the toxic sites.

In 1993, Turkmenistan joined the other four Aral Sea basin countries— Kyrgyzstan, Kazakhstan, Uzbekistan, and Tajikistan—in forming the International Fund for Saving the Aral Sea. Together, the nations have been working on cooperative efforts to deal with the enormous environmental problems of the Aral Sea basin.

THE CASPIAN SEA

With 1,098 miles (1,768 km) of coastline on the Caspian Sea, Turkmenistan has a critical interest in the health of that body of water. The Caspian is a unique ecological system unto itself and is subject to its own environmental pressures. Pollution, overfishing, overdevelopment, and the incursions of the oil and gas industries have all had adverse effects on the sea and its wildlife.

INTERNET LINKS

https://www.bbc.com/future/article/20180719-how-kazakhstan-brought-the-aral-sea-back-to-life
This article about the Aral Sea crisis includes many photographs.

https://earthobservatory.nasa.gov/world-of-change/AralSea
This website features pictures of and facts about the shrinking Aral Sea.

https://www.ozy.com/true-and-stories/how-turkmenistan-saved-its-golden-horse/89483
This article traces the history of the Akhal-Teke breed.

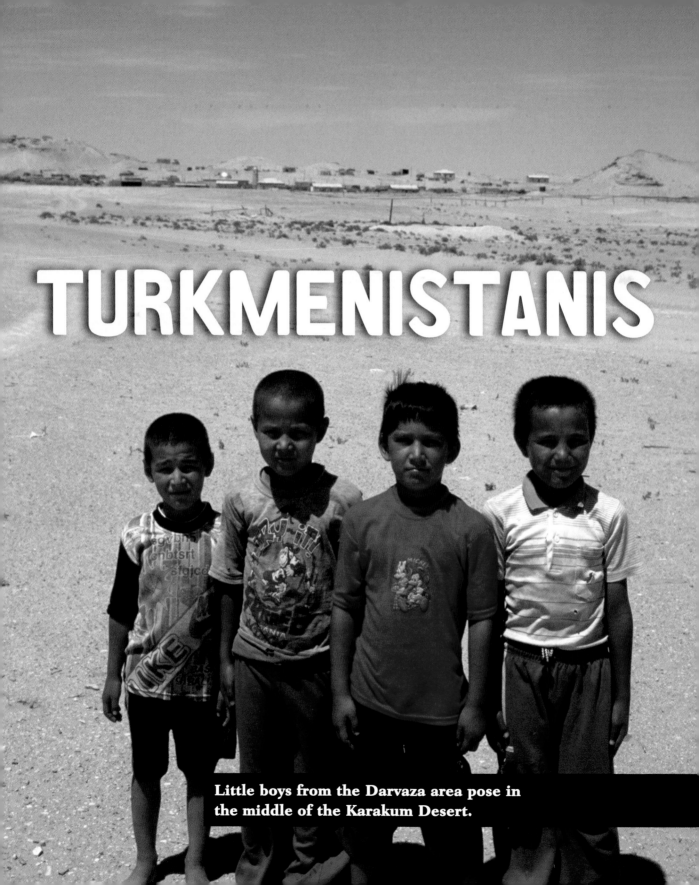

TURKMENISTANIS

Little boys from the Darvaza area pose in the middle of the Karakum Desert.

THE CITIZENS OF TURKMENISTAN
are Turkmenistanis, though they are
often referred to as Turkmen (or
Turkmens). Technically, however, Turkmen
is an ethnic group; people of that ethnicity
make up about 85 percent of the country's
population. (For English speakers, it helps
to remember that the suffix *-men* in this
case does not refer to the English word
"men," but rather it derives from Turkic,
meaning, essentially, "pure-blooded.")

Accurate demographic statistics for this country are difficult to pin down, since the government lacks transparency, freedom of information, and an independent media. Recent census results reporting falling national population numbers were said to be unacceptable to President Gurbanguly Berdimuhamedov, who allegedly asked for new methodology.

In July 2020, the population of Turkmenistan was estimated to be 5,529,000, but the CIA *World Factbook* and other sources added a caveat suggesting the total might be 1 million to 2 million lower because of large-scale emigration during the last decade or so. According to some sources, deteriorating economic conditions in Turkmenistan pushed upward of 1,879,400 people to seek work in other countries between 2008 and 2018. Their primary destinations were Russia, Turkey, and Ukraine. To stem that tide, the government reportedly began preventing people under age 40 from leaving the country.

6

In 2020, the net migration rate for Turkmenistan was estimated at -1.7 migrants per 1,000 members of the population. This negative figure indicates that more people emigrated from the country than entered it and placed the nation at number 161 out of 228 countries, in which lower rankings (228 being the lowest) indicate higher emigration rates.

Turkmen men wear traditional hats made of sheepskin.

Ethnically, the population of Turkmenistan is about 85 percent Turkmen, 5 percent Uzbek, and 4 percent Russian. There are also very small minorities of Armenians, Kazakhs, Tatars, Ukrainians, and others. It is a relatively young population, with the median age being about 29. (For comparison, the median age in the United States is 38.5.) Just over half of Turkmenistan's people live in urban centers, with about 47.5 percent living in rural settlements in the river valleys or the desert.

TRIBES, GROUPS, AND FAMILIES

Turkmen most likely came to Central Asia from the remote eastern steppes around 2,000 years ago. The people were part of the Oghuz tribes who settled in western Central Asia. Today, they live primarily in Turkmenistan, Uzbekistan, Iran, northern Iraq, and Afghanistan.

The main groups are the Yomud, from the western and northern parts of the country; the Teke, found today living around Ashgabat; and the Goklan, whose lands stretched to the west of Ashgabat. Historically, the nation's major tribes were independent of one another, each keeping to its own territory and maintaining a unique culture and distinct dialect. Interaction among the tribes led to shared traditions of art and jewelry styles. Still, each tribe distinguished itself from the others by retaining unique features and qualities, such as different weaving patterns and clothing styles, especially in terms of headgear.

The structure of the individual tribes was complex and varied somewhat in terms of leadership and authority, though urban, rural, and nomadic families alike showed great regard for their elders. Tribes were further divided into

A family sits outside their home in the northern part of Turkmenistan.

groups and then into extended families, the basic unit of social and economic organization. Most families were self-sufficient, living off the products of their livestock herds as well as a little farming.

Within the tribal system, women were the weavers and were responsible for milking the cows and sheep and preparing the dairy products so crucial to the family's diets. In settled communities, women also often helped plant and harvest crops. However, most important of all, they gave birth to and raised the children. Even today, a large family commands respect and admiration, which is why elaborate courting and wedding ceremonies are still among the most celebrated Turkmen social events.

Turkmen society was different from most other Muslim societies. Although Turkmen women were usually not visible participants in political affairs, they were never required to wear face veils or subject to strict seclusion. Their specialized and necessary roles and skills made them vital contributors to

Young women wear traditional red dresses adorned with embroidery in Ashgabat.

the economy, not just beneficiaries of it. Under Soviet rule, state ideology dictated equality between the sexes. Because of its Turkmen tribal traditions, the population of Turkmenistan was able to adjust to the major social change other cultures and societies found radical and offensive.

Still, during their years as citizens of a Soviet republic, Turkmen saw their culture trivialized, degraded, and ultimately replaced by rigid and uncompromising Soviet ideals. So encompassing was the communist ideology that uprooted the Turkmen way of life that the years since emancipation have been shaken by questions of identity and values.

Under President Saparmurat Niyazov, and continuing under Berdimuhamedov, the nation is discarding Russian influence and constructing a new national identity. This is being done largely through the promotion of myth, language, and customs, with both presidents being widely accepted as cultural authorities.

Statues of historical or legendary Turkmen heroes surround the lavish Independence Monument in Ashgabat.

The Russian Bazaar in Ashgabat is one of the largest covered markets in the country. It was built in the 1970s, during the Soviet era.

RUSSIANS

During the Soviet years, thousands of Russians relocated to Turkmenistan. Many were sent by the central government in Moscow to fill administrative, government, teaching, and other professional positions. Functioning in this capacity, they formed a prestigious and influential class of their own within the country of Turkmen. After the breakup of the USSR, the Russians were increasingly considered outsiders, though they held dual Russian and Turkmenistani citizenship. They were no longer welcomed by the new government, despite the fact that the government itself consisted largely of former Soviet leaders.

Niyazov, during his regime, wished to rid his country of people potentially disloyal to him. In 2003, he terminated the dual citizenship of the 100,000 remaining Russian-Turkmen, giving them 60 days to choose which affiliation they would keep. Rather than giving up their Russian citizenship or living as Russians in the Turkmen nation, many fled to Russia. Since then, Turkmenistan has become even less hospitable to its Russian population, banning all Russian media, removing Russian studies and language from its schools, and declaring college degrees granted from Russian institutions of higher learning—and in fact from all foreign universities—invalid.

INTERNET LINKS

https://www.cia.gov/library/publications/the-world-factbook/geos/tx.html
The CIA *World Factbook* has up-to-date demographic statistics for Turkmenistan.

https://www.rferl.org/a/escape-from-turkmenistan-almost-2-million-have-fled-but-the-president-won-t-hear-of-it/29987972.html
This report details the alleged government move to prevent citizens from leaving the country.

LIFESTYLE

A young man wears the national costume for a performance at the Kurban Bairam (Eid al-Adha) Festival in Ashgabat.

7

I'T'S NOT EASY TO GET A GOOD SENSE OF everyday life in Turkmenistan. The government strictly controls all avenues of information and only presents the images it wants seen. Like North Korea, the country is often called a "hermit nation" because it is so closed off from the rest of the world. That said, President Gurbanguly Berdimuhamedov wants to do business on an international scale and also wants to attract tourism. Accordingly, the country is promoted as a robust, healthy, happy place. However, the ambition to be a big player in the world and yet remain secretive and isolated is a tricky balancing act. So far, Berdimuhamedov has managed to keep complete control on the situation, and the nation is a pocket of stability in a volatile region.

On the subject of education, President Gurbanguly Berdimuhamedov has said, "Our main task is to grow a highly educated generation of true patriots who know the history of the people, take pride in today's high achievements of their country and strive to multiply the glory of independent Turkmenistan."

MEDIA AND HUMAN RIGHTS

All media outlets in Turkmenistan are strictly under the control of the government, which funds radio and television stations and owns all printing facilities. Editors of all newspapers and magazines are appointed by the president, who also directs their editorial content. Newspaper stories consist, for the most part, of the president's speeches and proclamations and the glorification of his various deeds and achievements. What space remains is filled with positive stories about holidays and Turkmen who display the attitudes and attributes that the president wishes to promote. Foreign newspapers and magazines were banned in 2002, and shipments are often confiscated at the borders.

The internet is highly censored, and only about 18 percent of the population goes online. International social networks are often inaccessible, and all foreign news sites are blocked.

The 692-foot (211 m) high Turkmenistan Broadcasting Center, built in 2011, sits high in the Kopet-Dag mountain range.

Turkmen like watching television; all channels are state-owned. About 10 percent of the programming is news, which consists entirely of material promoting the programs and ideologies of the government. The rest of the schedule is filled with folk music performances and patriotic programs. Russian programming is strictly limited and censored, and it consists mainly of children's shows. Some people have satellite reception to access Russian broadcasts, but this is considered risky. The government regularly seizes satellite dishes.

Journalists, both Turkmenistani and foreign, who contradict government expectations can expect harassment for themselves and their families and may experience difficulty in obtaining visitors' visas. In more extreme cases, arrests, torture, physical attacks, and other forms of intimidation have forced many journalists to stop working.

In 2020, Reporters Without Borders (RSF) called Turkmenistan an "ever-expanding news black hole." In its annual World Press Freedom Index, it rated the country at 179 out of 180, raising it one point from the previous year, in which it garnered the absolute bottom place on the scale. In 2020, only North Korea rated a lower score. Indeed, Turkmenistan is often compared to North Korea, which is usually considered the world's most repressive country.

Corroborating the RSF report, the international organization Human Rights Watch detailed a long list of concerns, saying, "The Turkmen government's dire human rights record saw no improvements in 2019. Turkmenistan remains an isolated and repressive country under the authoritarian rule of President Gurbanguly Berdimuhamedov and his associates." Amnesty International concurs, stating, "Turkmenistan remains effectively closed to human rights monitors and other international monitors. It is very difficult to verify the true extent of human rights violations, due to difficulties in accessing reliable information from within the country and the fact that the country remains closed to international scrutiny."

With those reports in mind, the lifestyle topics for this country can be based only on limited information.

Monuments throughout the city of Ashgabat, such as this tower in a traffic roundabout, glorify national power.

A shepherd on a donkey herds a flock of sheep in the Karakum Desert.

FAMILY STRUCTURE

The extended family is the central social unit of Turkmen society. People usually marry quite young, often in their teenage years. Traditionally, the groom's family pays a bride-price in the form of either animals and goods or cash to the bride's family. The woman leaves her family to live with her husband's family in his father's household. When a man is in his 30s, he leaves his father's household with his wife and children and forms a household of his own. He takes with him part of his father's wealth and establishes his own independent livelihood.

A man's work, in nomadic and rural settlements, takes him away from home quite often. His responsibilities center on farming, caring for livestock (including sheep shearing), and going to the market. A woman's work includes child care, food preparation, and the spinning, dying, and weaving of wool.

HOMES

Turkmenistan is a country of cities as well as rural settlements. The cities, many of them built in their present form under Soviet rule, have housing typical of the former Soviet republics. Large, block-style apartment buildings, as well as single-family mud-brick houses are common sights in the smaller towns. Palatial buildings line the streets of the neighborhoods of Ashgabat where government officials make their homes and their fortunes.

For centuries, though, the nomadic lifestyle of the Turkmen dictated a very different kind of residence. Living alternately in areas of extreme heat and extreme cold, the people needed shelter that would suit both climates and be portable as well. Their land had few trees for building houses, and stones and mud bricks were not very portable—hence, the yurt: a portable dwelling, circular in shape, and about 16 feet (4.9 m) in diameter. Its collapsible walls and roof are standard shelter for nomads, and even settled Turkmen often

The white buildings of Ashgabat gleam against the Kopet-Dag mountain range.

Everything the nomadic Turkmen owned or needed had to be moved at least twice a year and unpacked, reassembled, or installed on arrival at the new location. Decorative objects were a luxury, so weavers made practical, everyday items such as sacks, packs, rugs, and pillows beautiful as well as useful.

The woven bag was a staple of the Turkmen household, usually highly specialized according to its size and use. There were bags for carrying tobacco, spindles, tent poles, tea, flour, seeds, and bread. Bags hung on both sides of camels and horses, toting bedding, clothing, and pots.

Besides bags, the yurt was furnished with carpets. The dirt floor of the yurt was covered first with felted rugs that formed a soft, warm surface for people to walk and sit on. The inside walls were lined with woven carpets that served as decorations by day and bedding by night.

Under the high central opening, which allowed air to circulate, was a stove used to prepare food for the family and to heat the yurt in winter. In front of the stove, a specially shaped rug kept sparks from falling on the other rugs and coverings. The stove was framed with mud bricks or wood in a square 3 feet (0.9 m) on each side. Radiating from the stove, the interior of the yurt was divided into four sections.

This typical desert dwelling suits the nomadic lifestyle.

Near the doorway in the front of the yurt, people left their shoes, tied up small animals, stored stools, and received ordinary guests. Behind the stove was the family's sleeping area and the place where they received guests of distinction. There, the family stored or hung on the wall the main carpet—a pile (or tufted) rug that they unrolled when they had guests. Most other rugs in a yurt were flat-woven coverings. At night, the family slept in a row along the back of the tent. The men slept on one side and the women on the other, all on their own sleeping felts, covered with their own quilts, their heads pointing toward Mecca.

The work area for men was on one side of the stove; the women's work area was on the other. Both were furnished mostly with the equipment needed for the various tasks they performed. Depending on the tribe, the assigned side for each sex could be to the left or to the right of the central roof opening.

The women's side was known as the pot side, and all supplies needed for cooking were stored on posts or trestles high above the ground. Other supplies such as sheers, spoons, and bedding were laced to the walls in bags specially designed for them. One bag held dirty clothes, and another stored clean clothes.

The men's side was known as the provisions side. There, the family stored salt, grain, rice, and other dry foods in paired bags that hung on both sides of the camels during travel. Newly shorn fleeces and unused tent felts were stored on the men's side as well.

keep a yurt for summer living. The latticework walls of the simple structure are covered with felt or reed screens to create an impromptu home.

THE MARKET

Traditionally, the people of Central Asia did their buying and selling in outdoor markets, not in stores housed in permanent structures. The markets were usually temporary but scheduled, and people traveled at regular intervals to trade their wares. Today, the remnants of these huge markets are still active in some towns and villages. One market, the Tolkuchka, located outside Ashgabat, is typical of this traditional market style. Open Sundays and Thursdays, it is a place where Turkmen jewelers and weavers come to sell their wares to countrymen and visitors alike, haggling with them all in turn.

EDUCATION

One benefit inherited from the Soviet-era educational system is that nearly 100 percent of the population is literate. However, the system has undergone substantial revision since independence. Under President Niyazov, the requirement for attendance declined from 11 to 9 years, though in reality few children attended even that long. The school year was shortened, and even today the schools are closed during the cotton harvest so that children, teachers, and administrators can work in the fields.

All classes are taught in the Turkmen language; Russian has been removed from the curriculum along with all books written in Russian. Under Niyazov, the main textbook in all classes was his own book of moral principles and mythologized history, the *Ruhnama*. The schools themselves are crowded and largely unheated. Teachers are not well paid or qualified, and they must provide their own classroom supplies, such as pencils and paper, and any other texts they wish to use.

Students examine a world map at a school in Ashgabat.

The best way to assess a nation's general health is by examining certain statistical indicators and comparing them to those of other countries. One of the primary measures used is "life expectancy at birth." This figure is the average number of years a person born in a certain year can expect to live, if mortality factors remain constant. (However, these factors don't remain constant over time, so this statistic is hypothetical.) Since this figure is an average of all life spans within a given framework, it cannot predict any specific person's length of life.

Life expectancy at birth is used to compare conditions in different countries, but it also reflects trends up or down within any given nation. Just as longer life tends to correspond to better overall health in a population, it also aligns with overall quality of life. Therefore, the statistic is valuable in determining, in general, the level of a people's living standards.

In Turkmenistan, the life expectancy in 2020 was estimated to be 71.3 years—68.2 years for men and 74.5 years for women. This figure is relatively low, ranking the country at number 162 in the world, out of 228. That means people in 161 nations can expect to live longer lives than Turkmenistanis. The life expectancy has improved some since 1960, when it was close to 54.5 years, but it's still a long way from Japan's 2020 expectation of 86 years.

President Gurbanguly Berdimuhamedov has since sought to modernize the education system, according to his own dictates. In 2019, the Ministry of Foreign Affairs stated online, "In Turkmenistan large-scale work is under way in order to modernize the national educational system, develop university science and raise it to the level of the developed states." This undertaking includes the "intensive" construction of new children's preschool establishments as well as some new secondary schools, as well as the introduction of digital communication technologies into the classroom, with an increased focus on science. In keeping with the president's interest in health and fitness, emphasis is also being put on education and sport, "in order to further develop mass physical education and sport of the high achievements, improve the training methods for high-level specialists, masters of sports, qualified trainers."

Additionally, the study of foreign languages—the "deep study of English, French, German, Japanese and other languages"—has been brought back into the curriculum, after being discouraged under the Niyazov regime.

The president is also looking to increase attendance at the nation's universities. In 2019, according to the ministry, 12,242 students entered college, an increase of nearly 4,000 over the previous year. The same year, 9,063 students attended vocational or professional schools.

HEALTH CARE

Health care in Turkmenistan is free for all citizens, but the situation is far from satisfactory. In 2005, President Niyazov ordered all of the hospitals located outside the capital to be closed. Under Soviet rule, poorly trained workers and underused health-care facilities burdened the economies of its republics. These republics have struggled to pay for health care since independence. Turkmenistan's solution has lowered costs, but it has also reduced the availability and quality of services. Claiming that health-care workers suffered from a mindset that valued self-interest over service, Niyazov fired 15,000 trained nurses and doctors in 2004, and he replaced them with individuals drafted into the military. The government also prohibited workers from reporting cases of infectious disease. Turkmenistan's medical laboratories and treatment facilities were outdated even in the cities and are still not available in many rural areas. The death rates of mothers and children under the age of 5 were the highest in all of Central Asia during Niyazov's regime.

By 2018, President Berdimuhamedov had reportedly brought the level of health care up to world standards, according to the Ministry of Foreign Affairs. He did reopen hospitals outside of the capital city; the ministry reports there are 122 hospitals across the nation, most of them in the countryside.

PANDEMIC DENIAL   However, the government's claims were put to the test in 2020, when the coronavirus pandemic spread around the world. As the virus spread in March, Turkmenistan closed its border and suspended all international flights. People who wore masks in public were fined for "trying to create a panic," but in July, that approach was reversed and masks became

mandatory. However, the official reason given for the mask requirement and social distancing advisory was "dust." Meanwhile, President Berdimuhamedov recommended, without scientific evidence, the fumigating of public areas with the smoke of a certain herb to fight diseases in general.

Although, as of fall 2020, the government has continued to insist that there hasn't been a single instance of COVID-19 in the country, anecdotal reports suggest otherwise. Apparently there has been a great increase in cases of "acute respiratory disease or pneumonia of unknown cause."

This denial of the pandemic reflects a similar response to the HIV/AIDS epidemic, which Turkmenistan claims never occurred in the country.

In July 2020, women in Ashgabat wear masks in public to protect against "dust" in the midst of the global coronavirus pandemic.

MILITARY SERVICE

In 2019, the Armed Forces of Turkmenistan were estimated to have approximately 33,000 active troops in the national army; 500 in the navy; and 3,500 in the

air defense forces. All men are required to serve 2 years in the military once they turn 18. More than 100,000 men are drafted each year. Besides military service and training, conscripts are required to perform much of the work usually done by hired workers, such as road building and repair, health care, and harvesting (especially cotton). Since 2010, the leading arms suppliers to Turkmenistan have been China, Italy, Russia, and Turkey.

Turkmenistan also maintains an internal security system. Though its size is secret, its effects are substantial, and people live under the assumption that their activities are being monitored.

Servicemen take part in a military parade in Ashgabat on the anniversary of Turkmenistan's independence.

DRESS

The typical Turkmen woman wears a long dress called a *koynek*. It is a nearly floor-length garment often made of silk woven on narrow looms. Because the fabric is so narrow, the dress is cut straight with full-length triangular inserts in the middle, giving the dress a graceful flair at the bottom. The circular neckline is decorated with contrasting embroidery in brightly colored silk. The embroidery is usually done by the woman who owns the dress or by her mother as part of her dowry. Under the koynek, the woman wears pants called a *balak*, sometimes made of several kinds of fabric. Only the silk-embroidered bottom border of the balak shows beneath the koynek. A woman always has her hair pulled back, often in braids, and covered by a scarf. For special occasions, she will typically put on an elaborate headdress that shows off the jewelry that constitutes her family's wealth.

A Turkmen man will often wear loose-fitting blue trousers stuffed into tall, heavy boots. Over this, he traditionally wears a white shirt covered by a heavy silk jacket with red and golden stripes. A man's hat will often reveal what tribe he belongs to, and the most commonly seen style looks like an explosion of fluffy wool.

Traditionally, people remove their shoes before entering a yurt, whose inhabitants walk, sit, and sleep on the felted rugs that cover the floor. Indoors, individuals wear knitted slippers or socks called *joraps*. Usually made of soft lamb's wool, but sometimes of silk or cotton, the socks are usually covered with geometric or floral designs representative of a particular area.

Young people have been inclined to dress in Western-style clothing. Long hair, piercings, and gold teeth have been popular. However, President Niyazov disapproved of such styles and fashions, and he urged young people to dress in traditional clothing. President Berdimuhamedov has been more willing to embrace international standards in dress. However, modesty, especially for women, remains very important. Turkmen women would never be seen strolling down the street in shorts and a crop top.

INTERNET LINKS

https://www.advantour.com/turkmenistan/traditions.htm
This travel site has some information on traditions in Turkmenistan, including dress styles.

https://www.cia.gov/library/publications/the-world-factbook/geos/tx.html
The CIA *World Factbook* provides statistical information on lifestyle matters.

https://www.hrw.org/world-report/2020/country-chapters/turkmenistan
Human Rights Watch details Turkmenistan's authoritarian rule.

https://rsf.org/en/turkmenistan
This is the Reporters Without Borders page for Turkmenistan.

RELIGION

The grandiose Turkmenbashi Ruhy Mosque is the largest mosque in Central Asia.

8

TURKMENISTAN IS A SECULAR nation with a predominantly Muslim population. Unlike most Arab nations, where Islam permeates all aspects of life, Turkmenistan keeps religion separate, where it plays an important but not overarching role in daily life.

Freedom to worship in Turkmenistan is guaranteed in the constitution. Article 18 of Section 1 states, "The state shall guarantee freedom of religion and belief, and equality before the law. Religious organizations shall be separate from the state, their interference in the state affairs and carrying out the state functions shall be prohibited. The public education system shall be separate from religious organizations and secular." Further into the document, Article 41 states, "Each person shall independently determine his/her attitude toward religion, shall have the right to, individually or jointly with others, profess any religion or none, to express and disseminate beliefs related to attitude toward religion, to participate in religious observances, rituals, and ceremonies."

However, like many constitutional rights in Turkmenistan, freedom of religion is not as free in practice as it appears on paper. The law states that religious groups must register with the government. The only religions whose registrations have been accepted are Sunni Islam and Russian Orthodox Christianity. People wishing to take part in unregistered religions are forbidden to gather publicly, distribute materials, or recruit new members. The government's interpretation of "public gathering" prevents meeting privately as well.

The Turkmenbashi Ruhy Mosque is the resting place of former president Saparmurat Niyazov, who called himself Turkmenbashi. He had it built from 2002 to 2004 in his hometown of Gypjak, about 7 miles (11 km) northwest of Ashgabat. He died two years later and is now buried there. The building is as much a monument to himself as it is to Islam.

Religious intolerance in Turkmenistan links directly to the country's Soviet past, in which religion was banned for decades. As an atheist state, the Soviet Union deemed religion and communism to be incompatible. Though independence brought a revival of Islamic religious practice, Presidents Niyazov and Berdimuhamedov have both rigidly controlled the freedom of expression and worship in the country. Such control is quite foreign to Turkmen tradition, which, though overwhelmingly Islamic, has been notably tolerant and uninvolved in controlling or regulating the religious beliefs of others.

Niyazov built the Turkmenbashi Ruhy Mosque, reportedly the largest mosque in Central Asia, in his hometown of Gypjak, in central Turkmenistan. Even before its opening, the mosque had become controversial because quotes from Niyazov's *Ruhnama* adorned the walls with as much prominence as quotes from the Quran.

Similarly, Berdimuhamedov built the magnificent Gurbanguly Hajji Mosque, named for himself, in Mary. It was completed in 2009.

The Gurbanguly Hajji Mosque is named for the president of Turkmenistan. In 2018, its main dome was painted gold.

ISLAM

By far, most Turkmen identify themselves as Sunni Muslims. A tiny minority are Shia Muslims, a separate branch of the religion. Sunni Islam is a form of the religion that dates back to the disciples of Muhammad, the founder of the religion. While in some countries Sunni Muslims are quite explicit and rigid in their beliefs about proper behavior and modes of worship, Turkmenistan's Muslims have had to be flexible in the past to survive the Soviet antireligious regime. Today, flexibility reigns as long as they share the teachings of their president in their mosques and incorporate them into their sermons.

Sunni Muslims believe in one God, Allah, whose word was conveyed to them by the Prophet Muhammad in what is today Saudi Arabia. Principles underlying the faith are referred to as the Five Pillars of Islam. The first pillar is the belief that there is no other god but Allah, the true God, and Muhammad is his messenger; the second pillar is a promise to pray to God five times per day; the third commits a believer to serving and helping the poor; the fourth requires Muslims to fast from dawn to sundown during the month of Ramadan; and finally, the fifth pillar is the expectation that all who are able to will travel to the holy city of Mecca in Saudi Arabia once in their lifetimes. This pilgrimage is called the hajj.

Four men pray in the courtyard of the ancient, reconstructed Hodja Yusuf Hamadani Mosque in Merv.

GOVERNMENT AND RELIGION

Despite the secular nature of Turkmenistan's government, it does not adhere to a distinct separation of church and state. The government involves itself in religious policy and determines which expression of Islam is acceptable in the interest of the state. That is, the government defines a "Turkmen Islam" that it considers compatible with the nation's cultural heritage—emphasizing, for example, the veneration of ancestors. Religious oppression in Turkmenistan,

This
1881 magazine
illustration shows
the seige of
Geok Tepe.

therefore, stems not from differences in spiritual belief but from a fear of opposition to government policies.

Wary of foreign interference, the Turkmenistani government particularly discourages certain Arab-style Islamic practices and sects, such as the ultra-fundamentalist Salafi Islam known as Wahhabism. Prevalent in Saudi Arabia, it's known as being an extremely strict interpretation of the religion. Some critics say the Turkmenistani government uses fear of terrorism as an excuse to suppress religious freedom.

The government also supports a limited contingent of pilgrims making the hajj. Paying for passage and accommodations, the government typically allows about 180 pilgrims to make the long trip each year. The pilgrimage begins at Geok Tepe, where the Russians massacred 15,000 people in 1881. Following a ritual meal, the pilgrims leave, accompanied by prayers for peace, stability, and prosperity in Turkmenistan, which they carry with them to Mecca.

However, in lieu of the hajj, which most Turkmenistanis will never be able or allowed to make, the government encourages shrine pilgrimage, or *ziyarat*. This involves visiting sacred sites, preferably local ones. One such site is the tomb of Sufi master Najmuddin Kubra in Konye-Urgench (another spelling of Kunya-Urgench) in present-day Turkmenistan. Sufism is a mystical form of Islam that emphasizes the inward search for God. Kubra lived under the 13th-century Khwarazmian dynasty, a Muslim dynasty that ruled much of Central Asia, Afghanistan, and Iran.

INTERNET LINKS

http://www.forum18.org/archive.php?country=32
This site publishes news articles relating to religious intolerance in Turkmenistan.

https://www.refworld.org/docid/58738ed74.html
This document by the religious freedom nonprofit group Forum 18 provides an in-depth look at the lack of religious freedom in Turkmenistan.

https://www.state.gov/wp-content/uploads/2019/05/TURKMENISTAN-2018-INTERNATIONAL-RELIGIOUS-FREEDOM-REPORT.pdf
The U.S. State Department published this International Religious Freedom Report for 2018.

LANGUAGE

Customers entering a supermarket in Dashoguz, Turkmenistan, are greeted by signs in their native language.

9

S*ALAM!* (SAH-LAM) "HELLO!"

Nähilisiň? Türkmençe bilýärmiň? "How are you? Do you speak Turkmen?"

Turkmen, the official language of Turkmenistan, is a member of the Turkic family of languages, a group that also includes Turkish and Uzbek, as well as Kazakh, Kyrgyz, and Uighur. Many of these languages are like dialects of the same language—with similarities in syntactical structure and vocabulary. Most Central Asians who speak one Turkic language can at least understand speakers of another.

Still, there is a great deal of variety, and the 6.7 million people who speak Turkmen use more than seven dialects, including Yomud, Teke, Salir, Goklan, Arsari, and Chowdur. Each is associated with a specific tribe. The Yomud and Teke dialects have contributed the most to the official language, which was standardized in 1920. Other influences come from Arabic, Persian, and Russian, from which words have been adopted and integrated into the Turkmen language over the years.

Turkmenistan is the geographical home and center of the Turkmen language, but more than a million of its speakers live outside the country. This is not surprising given the relatively recent establishment of borders often randomly dividing a previously nomadic population. Most people who speak Turkmen outside Turkmenistan live in Iran (with 719,000 speakers) and Afghanistan (with 1.5 million speakers). There are significant populations living in Turkey, Uzbekistan, and Pakistan as well.

THE STRUCTURE OF TURKMEN

The common order of words in a Turkmen sentence is subject-object-verb. Words acquire meaning and context through the addition of suffixes. Suffixes added to nouns indicate gender and number or whether the word is singular or plural. Suffixes added to verbs indicate tense. The language

In 2002, President Saparmurat Niyazov renamed the months and days (and some other words) because they had Russian origins. Some of the new names honored himself and his family. January, previously *Yanwar*, was renamed *Turkmenbashi*, his own adopted moniker. April, previously *Aprel*, was named *Gurbansoltan* after his mother. In 2008, Niyazov's successor reversed the changes.

has 9 vowels, with both long and short sounds, and 23 major and 2 minor consonants. The vowel sounds of the suffixes and root words are always both long or both short.

WRITTEN TURKMEN

As a written language, Turkmen has gone through many changes. From the 18th century until 1929, it was written using the Arabic alphabet, though little was actually recorded, and Turkmen was primarily an oral language. In 1929, an alphabet similar to and based on the Roman (or Latin) alphabet was introduced. The Unified Turkish Latin Alphabet, as it was called, was replaced by Cyrillic script (in which Russian is written) in 1940 to standardize Soviet communications. After independence, the country reverted to a form of the Latin alphabet. In Afghanistan and Iran, Turkmen is written using the Arabic script.

An enormous monument to the *Ruhnama* stands in Ashgabat. Every evening at 8 p.m., the cover opens and a recording plays a passage from the former president's book.

HISTORICAL AND CULTURAL SIGNIFICANCE

Tribal loyalties and tribal identification have historically formed the basis of the social and political structure of the Turkmens. The language of the Turkmens, with its dialects peculiar to each tribe but intelligible to all, was one of many ways—like the patterns in rugs and clothes—people used to associate an individual with a tribe or region. When the Russians conquered the tribes and imposed their rule, they also introduced their language and alphabet.

By the time the Soviet Union lost its power in 1991, most urban Turkmen spoke Russian, the language that government administration and business were conducted in. Children learned Russian in school in addition to Turkmen, which was considered an inferior language to be used by those with no ambition.

Still, as late as 1979, more than 99 percent of Turkmen claimed and regarded Turkmen as their first language. One of the first acts of the new government in 1991 was to proclaim Turkmen as the national and official language.

Since 1991, political considerations have continued to strengthen the position of the Turkmen language as Russian influence slowly eroded. Once, Russian television and radio stations and publications encouraged the use of the Russian language. The Soviets had installed Russian officials in many government and teaching positions. These people found themselves unwelcome after the Soviet collapse, and many left the country. Today, Russian broadcasts and publications are banned or severely discouraged, and classes are conducted entirely in Turkmen. Until 1991, there were universities and training schools in Turkmenistan operating in Russian, but these have been shut down. It has been difficult to reopen these schools with Turkmen as the operating language because there are few scholars educated in Turkmenistan. Today, about 12 percent of Turkmen speak Russian as a first language.

INTERNET LINKS

https://glosbe.com/en/tk
This online dictionary will translate English to Turkmen or vice versa.

https://omniglot.com/writing/turkmen.htm
This site offers an introduction to Turkmen.

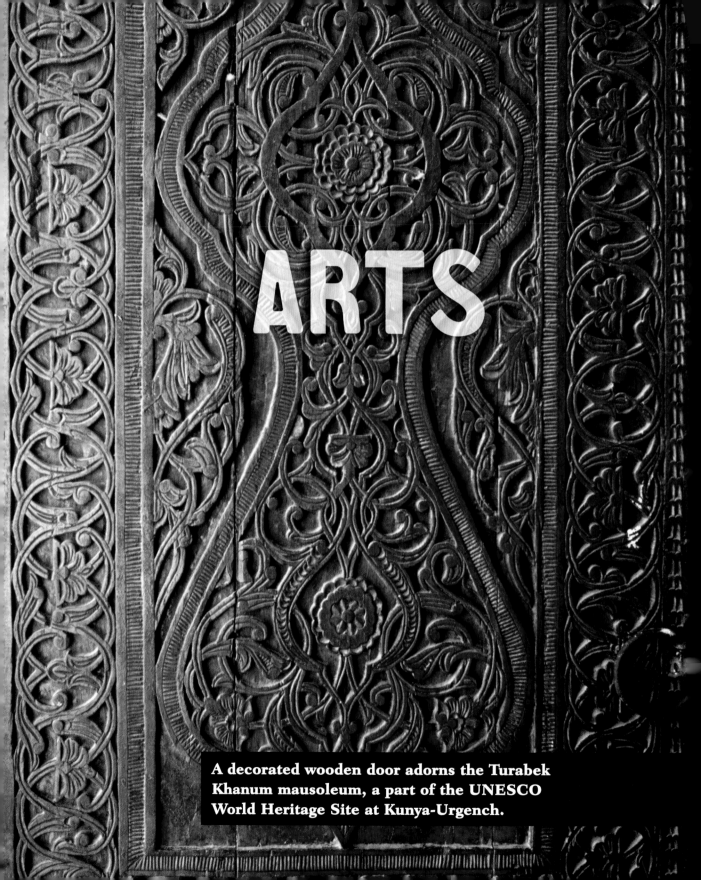

ARTS

A decorated wooden door adorns the Turabek
Khanum mausoleum, a part of the UNESCO
World Heritage Site at Kunya-Urgench.

10

THE ARTS OF TURKMENISTAN reflect the experiences of its people, from ancient times to today. Those experiences, in turn, have been shaped by geography, heritage, technology, the incursions of other cultures, and politics. From prehistoric times, the arts in Turkmenistan have been integrated seamlessly into daily life. Weavers, metalworkers, and potters made items that were both beautiful and essential to survival. Today, many of these traditional arts continue to be practiced, though selling or trading has expanded the range of items once produced solely for domestic use. Music and literary arts are also closely intertwined, with poems and epics preserved in song.

President Gurbanguly Berdimuhamedov enjoys singing to his people. In December 2018, the leader performed a song called "Dream" with his teenaged grandson Kerimguly and a backup band in celebration of the upcoming new year. The president wrote the lyrics, Kerimguly wrote the tune, and they performed the song in three languages. Berdimuhamedov and his grandson have also released a rap video.

THE TURKMEN CARPET

The most acclaimed art form of the Turkmen is the woven carpet, which is listed with UNESCO as one of the country's elements of "intangible cultural heritage of humanity." Knotted pile or flat weave, the rugs and bags were traditionally created by women on horizontal looms set up in yurts. Wealthy families might have an entire yurt set up for weaving. Sheep were sheared in spring, and most families wove only the wool obtained from their own sheep. During the weaving season, women would spin the wool into yarn, dye it, and then spend almost all their time at the loom. They wove their patterns from memory, without charts or diagrams, often nursing their babies and instructing their older daughters in the weaver's art as they worked. Families that wove items for sale at a local market usually produced two rugs in a season. A young woman without children or other responsibilities could weave about 1 square foot (0.09 sq m) in a 12-hour day. In wealthy families, for whom

INTANGIBLE CULTURAL HERITAGE

Just as UNESCO (the United Nations Educational, Scientific and Cultural Organization) works to protect natural and cultural World Heritage Sites, it also identifies examples of "intangible cultural heritage of humanity" that need to be preserved. These include, according to the group's website, "traditions or living expressions inherited from our ancestors and passed on to our descendants, such as oral traditions, performing arts, social practices, rituals, arts, festive events, knowledge and practices concerning nature and the universe or the knowledge and skills to produce traditional crafts."

The Convention for the Safeguarding of the Intangible Cultural Heritage has listed four entries for Turkmenistan: the traditional Turkmen carpet, the Kushtdepdi rite of singing and dancing, the spring holiday of Nowruz, and the epic art of Gorogly.

Turkmen women in traditional dress craft handmade carpets during a Nowruz celebration in Ashgabat.

A woman weaves an intricate design on a traditional carpet.

weaving was not an economic necessity, young women learned the skills and patterns that were part of their heritage as they wove the materials for their dowry and wedding ceremony.

No written account records the history of weaving, but archaeological evidence has suggested that weaving communities existed among some Turkmen tribes. Workers spun, dyed, and wove for the market that was created by the travelers and traders shuttling back and forth along the Silk Road. Within these communities, men sometimes wove as well, and each worker specialized in one part of the process instead of working from sheared wool to finished carpet.

The Soviet years were a time of great change for the carpet weavers of Turkmenistan. To promote Soviet ideals, officials compelled the weavers to adopt a pictorial style that would portray and glorify the heroes and events key to the development of communism. These carpets, known as theme or portrait carpets, were meant to be hung, rather than laid on the floor, and have deep, complex borders along their lower edges.

Factories in Ashgabat turned out countless carpets with Russian revolutionary Vladimir Lenin's portrait. Fidel Castro (the leader of Cuba), cosmonaut Yuri Gagarin, and Russian writers Alexander Pushkin and Maxim Gorky were rendered in tufted wool as well. In addition to Russians and key communist figures, however, the weavers commemorated Turkmen literary giants, including Fragi Makhtumkuli, Kemine, and Mollanepes. Scenes portraying historical events and Soviet ideals, such as solidarity among workers, also became central themes, taking their place throughout the Soviet Union.

In Ashgabat, people can visit a carpet factory where 200 workers weave the traditional Bukhara carpet, known throughout the world for its dark red beauty and its extensive patterning. Visitors can watch the rug makers tying the tiny knots that form the dense pile that has softened the footfall of wealthy collectors and kings. Ashgabat is also the site of the Carpet Museum, the permanent home of many beautiful carpets made in Turkmenistan, including the largest carpet in the world, which once graced the stage of the Bolshoi Ballet in Moscow. There, it hung as a backdrop to the dancers, reaching the height and width of the stage. Some of the portrait rugs that Turkmenistan's weavers produced during the Soviet years are also highlighted in the Carpet Museum, though many disappeared when Turkmenistan became independent.

The Bukhara carpet is the most famous of Turkmen designs, though it is named for the market where it was most often sold, in present-day Uzbekistan, rather than for the people who made it. Its main design element is the gul, the octagonal figure repeating across the width and length of the rug. Each tribe has its own signature gul and uses its hereditary gul in its weavings. Many carpets have two gul designs, one larger than the other and both repeating throughout the carpet. Guls identifying the five Turkmen tribes are featured on the flag of Turkmenistan.

FELTED RUGS

Though the rugs most often associated with Turkmenistan are woven, the most practical, and therefore the most commonly used, floor rugs are not woven, but felted. Used as bedding as well as floor coverings, these rugs are called *keshme*. For centuries, women made keshme for their families, and the rugs are still made in much the same way today as they were then.

Camel's or sheep's wool provides the raw material for the keshme, and women provide the labor and artistry. Before a sheep is shorn, it is washed to remove as much dirt from its fleece as possible. After the shearing is complete, the women lay the fleece on the ground and beat it with sticks to remove any remaining dirt and to separate the fibers. When it is clean and separated, they dye it in batches in the colors that they will need for their designs. Traditionally, the dyes were made from plants and insects according to old recipes. Today, the dyes are more likely to be commercially prepared from chemicals.

Ready for felting, the wool is then laid on a reed or straw mat in layers. The bottom layer is often undyed wool that is either dark or light, depending on the natural color of the sheep. On top of this, the women place tufts of dyed fleece in a pattern, building up the surface layer by layer until the design is complete.

The felting process is ancient and simple. Hot, soapy water is sprinkled on the wool until the piece is completely soaked. Then, the rug-makers roll up the

Women make a carpet from wool.

rug, straw mat and all. With their forearms pressing on the rug, they roll it back and forth to press out the water and to cause the wool to fuse to itself. Sometimes they unroll the rug; sprinkle it again with hot, soapy water; roll it up again; and press the piece some more. The resulting felted rug is strong, thick, and warm. The material is formed by the combination of heat, soap, and pressure in just the right proportions. The skills and the designs are passed on from one generation to the next.

Etiquette in a yurt requires that, before entering, people remove their shoes and put on slippers or socks. A felted rug provides a soft, warm surface to walk and sit on. The thickness of the rugs also provides some protection from the scorpions and snakes of the desert. Besides the keshme, Turkmens also use felted materials for clothing and for the walls of the yurts themselves.

JEWELRY

In a culture that did not rely on money as a source of wealth, jewelry was traditionally the Turkmen's way of displaying affluence and social status. The valuable objects belonged to each woman, and they were hers to inherit and pass

Traditional Turkmen jewelry is displayed at the National History and Ethnology Museum in Mary.

on, hence keeping much of the family's wealth under her control. Silver and gold ornaments were also created to decorate horses and riding equipment, such as reins, bridles, whips, and saddles. Only the most dire of economic circumstances would cause a family to sell its jewelry. Unlike weaving, which was practical as well as attractive, jewelry making was an art practiced entirely for its beauty.

Most Turkmen jewelry is made of silver, often coated with a thin layer of gold and set with precious and semiprecious stones, especially carnelian, whose shades of red figure in so much of Turkmen art. Jewelers are typically men who have studied under older master jewelers to learn the techniques and patterns associated with their tribe. Artisans use designs exclusive to their tribes, with some using a wider range of stones and others doing without the gold coating altogether. Often, the stones and the designs carry meaning as well as beauty, symbolizing joy, hope, healing powers, or strength of character.

The jewelry that a woman wears depends on her marital status and the occasion. A single girl wears an embroidered cap that has silver bangles and a pointed top. A married woman wears a high headdress that shows what tribe she is from. It is often decorated with a curved beaten silver plate. The top of the headdress might be adorned with as many as 100 pieces of jewelry, with more hanging from the sides. The most elaborate jewelry is worn by a bride and includes a headdress, bracelets,

A woman protects herself from the sun as she offers a horse whip for sale at her jewelry stall at the Tolkuchka Bazaar in Ashgabat.

rings, necklaces, and silver bangles for her hair. A bride from a wealthy family might be wearing approximately 30 pounds (13.6 kilograms) of jewelry at her wedding. Usually, a bejeweled woman wears pieces with dangling bangles that jingle as she moves.

Each item of jewelry has a specific name. One common piece, worn for many different occasions, is the *asyk*, a silver amulet (charm) that can either be attached to a woman's braids so that it hangs down her back or worn on a necklace as a pendant. The asyk can vary in weight from just a few ounces of silver to more than 5 pounds (2.2 kg). Another piece, the *tumar*, is a triangular bracelet worn high on a woman's arm. The tumar has spiritual significance for Turkmens and often has a hollow tube for storing talismans.

This *asyk*, or women's back pendant, is made of gilded silver with a carnelian stone.

LITERATURE

The origins of Turkmen literature are in the songs (*destan*), fairy tales, and poems (*epo*) that were passed on by the *bakshi*, or singing storytellers, as part of the oral tradition that was common to many cultures in the region. The story of Koroglu is the oldest Turkmen song. *Koroglu* is an epic consisting of 209 verses. Selected verses are accompanied by music.

During most of the 20th century, Soviet-educated intellectuals dominated Turkmenistan's cultural life. Berdi Kerbabayev was probably the most prominent Soviet-Turkmen writer, with a number of poems, plays, and novels to his credit. His themes were highly supportive of Soviet policies, hence his great success during his lifetime.

On the other hand, Rakhim Esenov is a novelist and journalist who incurred the wrath of President Saparmurat Niyazov. He was arrested in 2004 as he tried to smuggle 800 copies of his banned historical novel *Ventsenosny Skitalets* (*The Crowned Wanderer*) into Turkmenistan from Russia. Its hero is Bayram Khan, a Turkmen poet, philosopher, and military hero of the 16th century. Written

The 18th-century Turkmen poet Makhtumkuli Feraghy (also spelled Magtymguly Pyragy) is considered a national treasure. Widely regarded as the founder of Turkmen poetry and literary language, he is celebrated with a national holiday in June (the date was changed in 2017 from its previous day in May) called the Day of Revival, Unity, and Poetry of Makhtumkuli. Although it is no longer a non-working holiday, it is still observed with poetry readings, lectures, exhibitions, and other festivities throughout the country.

A golden statue of Makhtumkuli is shown here.

Makhtumkuli's times and those of his fellow Turkmen were filled with conflict not of their own making. The poet saw his and his compatriots' suffering as the cruel gift of fate. In his lifetime, he witnessed the Turkmen tribes at the mercy of the warring empires—the armies from Iran, Bukhara, and Khiva (now part of Uzbekistan)—that swept through their territory numerous times. No matter who occupied their lands, the Turkmen were consistently considered the invading force's enemies. Villages were sacked and burned, men were massacred, and women and children were carted off as loot. Some cities, such as Mary, were destroyed and rebuilt several times, and dams and oases were repeatedly ruined, leaving behind famine and barren, desert-like conditions.

To Makhtumkuli, the world was a place of nightmares, where the clubs of the enslavers triumphed because of the disunity that reigned among the Turkmen tribes. He longed for a powerful confederation of tribes to throw off the burden imposed by the joint domination of the outsiders and warring native leaders. However, he never believed this hope would be realized, which was the ultimate source of his despair. He died without seeing the end of tribal warfare and the ousting of the foreign invaders. Yet his voice spoke to his people, and as a poet writing in their language, he was heard by the largely illiterate Turkmen who could recite all of his poems by heart.

10 years earlier but banned because of what Niyazov called historical errors—that is, Khan was correctly portrayed as a Shia rather than Sunni Muslim—the novel was finally published in Russia in 2003. Esenov was charged with using the mass media to incite social, national, and religious hatred. The elderly author was imprisoned despite suffering a stroke following an interrogation. Unable to leave the country for medical treatment, Esenov's cause was championed by PEN International, a writers' organization for creative freedom, which worked for his release. In 2008, all charges against him were dropped.

Turkmenistani novelist and journalist Rakhim Esenov (*right*) speaks with American journalist Diane Sawyer (*left*) at the 2006 PEN Literary Gala at the American Museum of Natural History in New York City.

TRADITIONAL MUSIC

Turkmenistan's ancestral nomadic lifestyles led to the development of a strong bardic, or lyrical, musical tradition. Itinerant, or wandering, performers called bakhshi sang or recited verse, ballads, and oral tales, often to musical accompaniment. Today, that folk music is essential to many Turkmen festivities,

Many of President Niyazov's theories of life and his interpretation of Turkmenistan's history are contained in his two-volume work, Ruhnama, *or* Book of the Soul. *The first volume was published in 2001 and contains not only the author's own life story but also his version of Turkmenistan's history and the moral lessons to be learned from it. The second volume was published in 2004 and addresses family values and patriotism.*

Ruhnama *was required reading for all Turkmen during Niyazov's regime, and it is still regarded as a sort of holy book. Excerpts are inscribed over the doors and on the walls of mosques, as Niyazov declared it to be a sacred text to be studied and read alongside the Quran. It was the main text in all classrooms, where students read it at the beginning of every school day. In many classrooms, it was the only text. On Saturdays, adults were required to study the book as well and to contemplate spiritual matters.*

In 2005, a copy of the book was sent into space aboard a Russian booster rocket. In its container, adorned with the Turkmenistan flag, the book is reportedly going to orbit the earth for 150 years.

In 2013, Niyazov's successor Gurbanguly Berdimuhamedov removed Ruhnama *from*

Young women hold flowers and the *Ruhnama* book as they take part in Turkmenistan's 2007 presidential election at a polling station in Ashgabat.

Turkmenistan's public schools. He also lightened some other requirements, for example, declaring that the country's universities would no longer test applicants on their knowledge of the book. On the other hand, some of Berdimuhamedov's own writings have become part of the curriculum.

especially weddings. Age-old instruments define the sound, with the *dutar* being one of the most distinctive of them. The long-necked, two-stringed lute with a soft, pretty sound is popular throughout Central Asian folk music. Another string instrument is a *ghidjak*, which has a round body and a short, fretless neck. Unlike the dutar, which is strummed or plucked, the ghidjak is played with a bow. Traditional Turkmen music also makes use of the *tuiduk*, a clarinet-like wind instrument.

Traditional instruments are used in the performance of the epic art of Gorogly, one of Turkmenistan's celebrated entries on the UNESCO List of Intangible Cultural Heritage. This oral tradition describes the achievements of the legendary hero Gorogly and his 40 cavalrymen. The epic incorporates narration, singing, composition, prose, poetry, and vocal improvisation, and it functions to pass on Turkmen culture to new generations.

Musicians perform on traditional instruments at a horse festival in Ashgabat.

The instruments are also a part of the performance tradition of Kushtdepdi (or Kusht Depdi). This rite of singing and dancing has been described as the national dance of Turkmenistan. As such, it is performed on all national holidays. The art involves creative vocal improvisation and dancing to convey good wishes and happy feelings.

The craftsmanship of dutar making, as well as its role in music performance, is nominated for addition to the UNESCO list in 2021.

PAINTING

The fine art of painting is not native to Turkmen folk culture, but during the Soviet era, a number of artists gained some prominence. Their work often features vivid colors and portrays a mix of Turkmen and Russian culture and style. Trained in Moscow in the European manner, these artists' works nevertheless reflect the landscapes, people, and folk styles of their own country.

An exhibition of the works of painter Durdy Bayramov was held in Toronto in 2014.

Chary Amangeldyev is one such artist who experimented with a range of painting styles and who is perhaps best known for his triptych painting *To the Light*. His brother Aman Amangeldyev was also an important Turkmenistani artist. Another esteemed 20th-century Turkmenistani artist is Durdy Bayramov, a prolific painter and photographer.

INTERNET LINKS

https://ich.unesco.org/en/state/turkmenistan-TM
This UNESCO page lists the intangible heritage elements of Turkmenistan, with links to more in-depth information, videos, and photographs.

https://www.metmuseum.org/toah/hd/turk/hd_turk.htm
This museum site looks at historical Turkmen jewelry.

https://pen.org/advocacy-case/rakhim-esenov
This literary human rights organization reports on the experience of writer Rakhim Esenov.

https://www.rferl.org/a/qishloq-ovozi-turkmenistan-makhtumkuli/25384568.html
This article is a thoughtful introduction to the life and work of Makhtumkuli.

http://simplyknowledge.com/popular/gk_detail/kusht-depdi
This page describes the national performance art of Kushtdepdi.

https://soviet-art.ru/soviet-turkmen-artist-chary-amangeldyev
This site presents the life and work of Chary Amangeldyev, with links to facts about Durdy Bayramov and other Soviet-Turkmen artists.

LEISURE

Men ride bikes on World Bicycle Day in Ashgabat on June 3, 2020.

11

THE HEALTH AND LEISURE activities of Turkmenistanis are a matter of great interest to the government. President Gurbanguly Berdimuhamedov, like his predecessor Saparmurat Niyazov, actively encourages his citizens to aspire to healthy living as both a patriotic and spiritual pursuit.

Encouragement, in this matter, is often enforced. Under Niyazov, citizens were required to read his book of life guidance. To advance his

In 2020, Turkmenistan inaugurated a new monument in honor of bicycles. The opening of the 98-foot (30 m) Bicycle Monument, located in the south of Ashgabat, was celebrated on June 3 with a mass bike ride led by Gurbanguly Berdimuhamedov.

spiritual agenda, Niyazov banned smoking, chewing tobacco, loud music coming from cars, and movies. Nightclubs were required to close at 11 p.m. Women were encouraged to wear the traditional, long, embroidered dresses and headscarves and reject Western styles of clothing. He also banned certain leisure and cultural activities, such as opera, ballet, and circuses, for being "un-Turkmen-like." (Berdimuhamedov would later reverse those particular restrictions.) Niyazov believed that higher standards of conservatism would better serve Turkmenistanis, who would then reap the rewards of spiritual superiority in the 21st century.

The concept of leisure as enjoyed by people on vacation or traveling for pleasure is new to most Turkmenistanis, who traveled mainly for economic and survival reasons and generally don't take vacations. Still, under the leadership of President Niyazov, who had a taste for lavish projects, the government developed some elaborate centers dedicated to leisure activities. Among other things, he built an ice palace in the desert where people can ice skate.

ALCOHOL USE

When it came to changing people's personal habits, though, the president was up against a challenge. Joblessness and drug abuse afflicted the young people of his country. Alcohol use had also become common among some people, particularly urban men. Though Islam forbids the use of alcohol, this is one of the areas where many Turkmenistanis subscribe to their own form of the faith. During the Soviet era, Russia's cultural influence brought a love of vodka to Turkmenistan, where it remains the preferred alcoholic beverage.

When Berdimuhamedov succeeded Niyazov as president in 2007, he continued on the same path of further restricting alcohol availability for matters of health. The government's influence appears to have had an effect. Alcohol consumption has been falling.

Of the five Central Asian nations, Turkmenistan ranked third for alcohol use, after Kazakhstan and Kyrgyzstan. From a global point of view, Turkmenistan's alcohol use ranked it at 107th in the world, much lower than most of Europe and Russia.

THE WALK OF HEALTH

During Saparmurat Niyazov's years as president, he oversaw a number of large construction projects in Ashgabat. One is the Walk of Health, also called the Serdar Health Walk, which is part of the Saparmurat Turkmenbashi Eternally Great Park. This concrete path, completed in 2005, runs along the high ridges of the treeless Kopet-Dag foothills outside the city. There are actually two paths—one an extremely grueling 23-mile (37 km) trek, the other a more manageable 5 miles (8 km). The walk is a footpath that is accessed by a staircase nearly 1 mile (1.5 km) long. A large white marble statue of President Niyazov dressed in a tracksuit inspires walkers as they get started, and various quotations of his posted along the way further encourage them. Walkers need to be tough; the long path provides no shade or water.

Niyazov used to require all government workers to walk the long path at least once a year. He encouraged all citizens to do the same. He himself was unable to hike the Walk of Health, as he had preexisting health conditions.

The grueling staircase to the Walk of Health is only the beginning of the long trek.

Supporters
arrive at the
Turkmenistan
National Football
Championship
match between
Altyn Asyr and
Kopet-Dag on
April 19, 2020.

SPORTS

Football, or soccer, came to Turkmenistan in the 1920s along with Soviet rule, and it remains the most popular sport in the country. With independence, the country created its own national team, which is a member of FIFA, the International Football Federation. Although the country has had only limited success on the world stage, it sponsors its own national championship with eight local clubs competing.

STUDENT AND WORKER SPORTS AND GAMES   Many of the nation's schools have teams for competitions in chess, volleyball, and tae kwon do. From these championships, it is possible for participants to go on to international competitions, especially in tae kwon do. Tournaments for tae kwon do featuring the winners of regional contests take place six times a year. Each tournament consists of 100 athletes taking part in three kinds of martial arts, competing for belts at all levels. Winners go on to take part in the contest for the World Martial

Arts Championship. Turkmenistan's place as an Asian culture is reflected in the popularity of martial arts such as karate and kickboxing, as well as tae kwon do. Table tennis is another popular sport in Asia that enjoys a large following in Turkmenistan.

Workplaces also form teams that compete in various games such as checkers and darts. Following a system of encouraging competition among labor collectives first established by the Soviets, workers compete within Turkmenistan, with the winners going on to face champions from other former Soviet republics.

THE OLYMPICS

Turkmenistan has high hopes for Olympic achievement. To that end, it has built an Olympic complex, despite never having hosted the games. It did, however, host the Asian Indoor and Martial Arts Games in 2017 when it opened. The $5-billion complex, containing 30 high-tech sporting venues, hotels, and other facilities, covers around 370 acres (150 ha) on the outskirts of Ashgabat.

This night view shows the Saparmurat Turkmenbashi Olympic Stadium and the Olympic village built for the 2017 Asian Indoor and Martial Arts Games.

Since 1996, Turkmenistan has sent athletes to the Olympic Summer Games, though none have yet won any medals. (It has yet to participate in a Winter Olympics, though that may change in the future.) In 2016, the Turkmenistani Olympic team sent nine athletes—four men and five women—to the summer games held in Rio de Janeiro, Brazil. There they participated in boxing, weightlifting, swimming, track and field, and judo. When the team returned empty-handed from Rio, President Berdimuhamedov publicly berated his government sports minister. Berdimuhamedov also serves as the president of the Turkmenistan Olympic Committee. (The 2020 Olympic Games in Tokyo were postponed because of the worldwide coronavirus pandemic.)

At the historic site of Nisa, horsemen attend a ceremony kicking off a 500-day nationwide horse race on May 5, 2016. The race was a countdown to the 2017 Asian Indoor Games, which took place in Ashgabat.

HORSE SHOWS

Horseback riding is a source of national and personal pride in Turkmenistan. Beautiful Akhal-Teke horses—an ancient breed from Turkmenistan's Karakum Desert, perform in competitions and races at many national events. As part of the competitions, students and their riding masters demonstrate the art of training horses and riders.

President Niyazov was a proud horse owner, and a picture of his prized steed, Yanardag, is on the national coat of arms. President Berdimuhamedov is also a big fan of horses and has proclaimed himself the "People's Horsebreeder." He is said to own hundreds of Akhal-Tekes, and he is often photographed on horseback.

PERFORMANCES

During festivals and on holidays, people all over Turkmenistan celebrate by watching dancers and listening to music. Many dance and music troupes travel around the country to different festivals and gatherings, performing traditional and contemporary dances, as well as reading, enacting, and singing songs from the Gorogly and other poems and myths, especially love poems. When the troupes perform, they wear beautiful traditional clothing and jewelry.

INTERNET LINKS

https://www.atlasobscura.com/places/walk-of-health
This is a short entry about the Walk of Health in Turkmenistan.

https://www.mfa.gov.tm/en/articles/10
This page from Turkmenistan's Ministry of Foreign Affairs details steps the country has taken to encourage sports and the health of the nation.

https://www.nationalgeographic.com/travel/destinations/asia/ turkmenistan/turkmen-horse-day-ashgabat-akhal-teke/
This short article about Horse Day in Turkmenistan includes photos of Akhal-Teke horses.

https://www.rferl.org/a/silly-dictator-turkmenistan-land-health-happiness/24945699.html
Radio Free Europe/Radio Liberty offers a look at President Gurbanguly Berdimuhamedov's efforts to encourage health and sports.

FESTIVALS

President Gurbanguly Berdimuhamedov, surrounded by officials and participants from the Asian Indoor and Martial Arts Games, poses with melons on Melon Day, August 18, 2017.

A YEAR IN TURKMENISTAN IS FULL OF various celebrations and observances. There's a day for celebrating melons, another day for honoring Turkmen carpets, and another day for appreciating national poet Makhtumkuli Feraghy. There are also the usual patriotic commemorations and religious holidays. Keeping track of these special days takes vigilance, though, as they are quite changeable, depending on the whims of whoever is in power at the time.

NEW YEAR'S DAY

Like most of the world, Turkmenistan celebrates New Year's Day on January 1. Festivities begin the day before on New Year's Eve. Tradition calls for people to dress in clean clothes, take out all the trash, clean the house, and return all items or money borrowed during the year. Most important, the family table should be loaded with festive foods. When all these matters are taken care of, Turkmenistanis are ready to welcome the new year, a critical observance, since custom states that the way you bring in the year will determine the way you will spend it.

12

In 1994, President Saparmurat Niyazov created Melon Day, a new official holiday. He was quoted as saying, "The Turkmen melon is the source of our pride. Its taste has no equals in the world. The smell makes your head spin." Although some of the former president's holidays were canceled by his successor, Melon Day remains a favorite public occasion, celebrated every second Sunday in August.

Guests arrive on New Year's Eve around 6 p.m. and may continue to arrive through the night as they make their rounds visiting friends and family. At midnight, everyone goes out into the yard to greet the new year with fireworks for the children and champagne for the adults. Some families have a New Year's tree decorated like a Christmas tree, but it is most likely an artificial one because trees are too scarce in Turkmenistan to be cut down for temporary decorations. Families and friends also give gifts to the children on this important day.

NOWRUZ

The spring festival of Nowruz, or Novruz Bairam, is a favorite throughout Central Asia. Nowruz means "new day," and though it is an Islamic festival of the vernal equinox, it includes elements and traditions that predate Islam. In fact, the holiday has very ancient roots. It is an occasion for dancing, traditional competitions and games, and music. Street fairs and parades are staged throughout the country.

In 2009, Nowruz was added to UNESCO's List of the Intangible Cultural Heritage of Humanity. In 2010, the United Nations declared March 21 the International Day of Nowruz.

NATIONAL HOLIDAYS

Virtually all nations observe patriotic holidays as a means of supporting a national identity. These days usually coincide with anniversaries of historic events. Turkmenistan's most important state commemorations are public holidays—for which government offices and businesses close, providing people with a day off from work and school. Other state observances are marked with ceremonies, but not as days off. Some of the most important national holidays are these:

CONSTITUTION DAY   May 18 is set aside to honor the nation's document of law. Since its adoption in 1992, the constitution has been amended seven times, most recently in 2016. The day is observed with a ceremony at the

Monument to the Constitution in Ashgabat, a tall, white marble building that was built from 2008 to 2011 to honor the 20th anniversary of the constitution. Festivities also include concerts and poetry readings.

EARTHQUAKE REMEMBRANCE DAY October 6 is the Day of Commemoration and National Mourning. It marks the catastrophic earthquake of 1948, which struck Ashgabat, causing an enormous loss of life—estimates are anywhere from 10,000—176,000—and leveled much of the city.

INDEPENDENCE DAY On October 27, 1991, Turkmenistan declared its independence from the Soviet Union. In 2017, the holiday was moved up a month to September 27, so as to coincide with the final day of the 10-day Asian Indoor and Martial Arts Games that were held in Turkmenistan that year. The change also reduced the public holiday from two days to one day. The

People release balloons during a military parade in Ashgabat marking Turkmenistan's Independence Day.

These are the public holidays in Turkmenistan. In addition, there are many observances, such as Melon Day on the second Sunday in August.

January 1 . . . . . New Year's Day

March 8 . . . . . . International Women's Day

March 21–22 . . . Nowruz (Spring holiday)

May 18 . . . . . . Constitution Day

September 27 . . . Independence Day

October 6 . . . . . Day of Commemoration and National Mourning (day of remembrance for the victims of the 1948 earthquake)

December 12 . . . Day of Neutrality

Changeable Muslim holidays:

Kurban Bairam (Eid al-Adha)

Khait (Eid al-Fitr)

holiday has remained on September 27 since then. Independence is celebrated throughout the country with parades and festivities.

DAY OF NEUTRALITY   In 1995, Turkmenistan declared itself a neutral country, unaligned with the interests, military or otherwise, of any other country. December 12 is now an important national day of celebration, marked by mass revelry and concerts.

Two other occasions commemorate historical events. On January 12, Turkmens mourn the day when their ancestors were defeated by the Russians at the Geok Tepe fortress in a clash that took thousands of lives. May 9 is called Victory Day, in honor of the defeat of the fascists and the German surrender in World War II. Both days were once public holidays but now are simply observances.

RELIGIOUS HOLIDAYS

As a predominantly Muslim nation, Turkmenistan celebrates the two most important religious holidays along with the rest of the Islamic world—Eid al-Adha, the Feast of the Sacrifice, and Eid al-Fitr, the Festival of Breaking the Fast. These events occur on different days each year, as they are determined according to the lunar Islamic calendar.

In Turkmenistan, Eid al-Adha is called Kurban Bairam. It commemorates the obedience of the biblical Ibrahim (Abraham), who was willing to sacrifice his son at God's command. The faithful will often sacrifice a sheep and prepare traditional foods for neighbors and relatives. On this holy day, Turkmenistanis also sail into the air on grand swings erected for this day, believing that swinging on Kurban Bairam will cleanse their souls.

Ramadan is the holiest month for Muslims, a solemn month of fasting and introspection. During the four weeks of Ramadan, people do not eat or drink from sunrise to sunset. Like Muslims throughout the world, Turkmen celebrate the end of the fasting season with magnificent feasts and parties with family and friends, beginning at midnight on Eid al-Fitr, or Khait. Dressed in their finest traditional clothing, people dine at elaborately laden tables until dawn. Music is heard throughout the land, and everyone joins in the dances or, at least, applauds the revelers.

INTERNET LINKS

https://www.officeholidays.com/countries/turkmenistan
This site provides a quick description of Turkmenistan's holidays.

https://www.timeanddate.com/holidays/turkmenistan
This calendar site provides the dates of annual public holidays and observances in the country.

FOOD

A man holds a large watermelon at a bazaar in Ashgabat.

13

THE CUISINE OF TURKMENISTAN IS much like that of the rest of Central Asia. It reflects the age-old diet of the nomadic peoples of the past as well as more recent influences of Russian tastes. Within the vast region of Central Asia, however, there are differences in diet, depending on geography and ethnic traditions.

For example, unlike some of its neighbors, where fish is uncommon, Turkmenistan has access to the Caspian Sea and the fish that live in it. The deserts of Turkmenistan, on the other hand, restrict agriculture in many areas, and crops need irrigation. Tomatoes, onions, carrots, and melons are used a great deal, along with rice and wheat. The diet is high in bread and cereal products such as noodles.

The favorite meat is lamb, but chicken, deer, camels, and wild game also supplement the diet. Unlike in Kyrgyzstan, the consumption of horsemeat is forbidden.

The Turkmenistani cuisine is not fancy; it's mostly basic stews and soups. It's also not highly seasoned, though cooks will use ground red or black pepper, mint, saffron, and azhgon—an aromatic seed—for flavor.

SACRED BREAD

Chorek, a type of thick, naan-like flatbread, is perhaps the most essential, revered food in the Turkmenistani diet. Round loaves are baked in a

President Saparmurat Niyazov reportedly abolished the Turkmen word *çörek* (or *chorek*), meaning "bread," and replaced it with the word *gurbansoltan*, his mother's name. He also named the month of April for her. When Gurbanguly Berdimuhamedov succeeded Niyazov as president, he reinstated the traditional words.

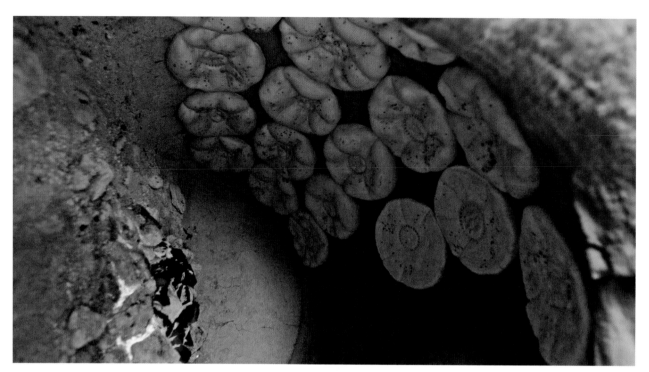

Loaves of bread bake on the sides of a clay oven called a *tamdyr*, or tandoor.

tamdyr (or *tandyr*), a clay oven, and are served with every meal. The tamdyr is considered the most sacred place in a house, and the chorek itself is treated with great respect. Etiquette rules govern the way chorek should be handled; for example, it's impolite to turn it upside down or drop it on the floor.

POPULAR DISHES

The everyday diet is heavy on meat, and lamb and mutton are the most favored. Beef, goat, and chicken are also used, but not pork. Being a predominantly Muslim people, Turkmenistanis abide by the Islamic dietary restrictions against eating pork. Lamb and other meats are roasted, skewered and grilled (*shashlyk*), stewed, or chopped into rice or noodle dishes, or they are mixed with vegetable fillings for dumplings (*manti*) and flatbreads.

One of the most common dishes is *ash*, or *plov*, a kind of rice pilaf found throughout Central Asia in various interpretations. The Turkmenistani version often features chopped carrots with chunks of lamb. Another typical meal is *shurpa* (also seen as *shorpa*), a meat and potato stew or soup. If Turkmenistan can be said to have a distinctive national dish, it would be *dograma*, a stew of shredded meat and bread.

Russian dietary influences, leftover from Turkmenistan's days as a Soviet republic, are seen in mayonnaise-based salads, cabbage rolls, and buckwheat groats. Russian dishes are more likely to be served in restaurants than at home. The Russian influence is also well ingrained in the love of vodka.

MELONS

Turkmenistan is well known for its melons, which are considered a national treasure. They are celebrated on Melon Day, a national holiday in August. The Day of the Turkmen Melon takes place on the second Sunday of August and features contests, sports competitions, and cultural events. Begun in 1994, the holiday is fairly recent, but melon growing is an ancient tradition in the region. Although the "Turkmenbashi melon," a large muskmelon, is praised as the country's most delicious fruit—it was named for former president Saparmurat Niyazov—there are many varieties of melon grown.

An abundance of melons are free for the taking after the annual Melon Day in August.

CRACKING DOWN ON ALCOHOL

When President Gurbanguly Berdimuhamedov set out to change his countrymen's relationship with alcohol, it was for health reasons, not religious ones. In 2019, new laws were passed that set strict restrictions on the selling and consumption of beer, wine, and hard liquor. Many locations, such as sports venues, public transportation, and city parks, were deemed off limits to alcohol. In addition, the legal drinking age was raised from 18 to 21. Beginning in 2012, the sale of any sort of alcohol became illegal on weekends, except for in bars and restaurants. On national holidays, the sale of alcohol is banned completely.

Berdimuhamedov, who himself is known to have diabetes, actively encourages citizens to live healthful lifestyles. He champions sports and exercise, and he has promoted mass activities to improve health and fitness as a matter of national pride.

DRINKS

Green tea (*chai*) is the main beverage, served hot, and usually without milk. In the Dashoguz region, the tea is sometimes served "Kazakh-style," with milk. That milk is usually not cow's milk, however, but more commonly sheep or camel milk.

A favorite milk-based drink is *chal* (or *chala*), a cold, sparkling beverage made from fermented camel's milk. Cow's milk is made into a sour, yogurt-like drink called *gatyk* and is often served for breakfast.

Although Muslim tradition forbids the drinking of alcoholic beverages, many Turkmenistanis take a casual, or perhaps cultural, approach to that dictate. Vodka is the most prevalent alcoholic beverage, along with beer, and the country also produces wines.

EATING AT HOME

The economy of Turkmenistan has not flourished enough to support many restaurants or the habit of dining out. However, eating is still a social event that brings families and clans together. Meals are shared on a decorative cloth (*sachak*) spread on the floor, with all dishes served at the same time and the family seated on floor cushions. Food is eaten either by hand or with cutlery, but always using the right hand only.

Preparing food gives women a chance to exchange news and teach their daughters how to prepare the dishes the family eats on a daily basis. Throughout the day, a kettle is kept boiling for tea, and visitors are offered tea and cookies if they drop in. While the guests sip their tea, the women prepare more food. No one leaves a Turkmenistani house without eating a meal.

Two men enjoy a lunch together at a rare restaurant in Turkmenistan.

INTERNET LINKS

https://caspiannews.com/news-detail/turkmenistans-top-10-dishes-2017-10-3-54
This site discusses 10 of the country's most popular dishes.

https://turkmenkitchen.com/en
This site supplies recipes for Turkmenistani dishes.

SHURPA (MEAT AND VEGETABLE SOUP)

2 pounds (900 grams) lamb on
  the bone
10 cups (2.4 liters) water (or
  chicken or beef broth)
1 teaspoon cumin
salt and pepper
1 cup (150 g) onions, chopped
1 ½ pounds (680 g) tomatoes,
  peeled and chopped
2 carrots, diced
2 green bell peppers, cut into
  bite-sized pieces
4 medium potatoes, peeled and
  cut into chunks
1 15-ounce (400 g) can chickpeas,
  drained and rinsed (optional)

Place the lamb in a large pot. Pour 10 cups of water over it, and bring the water to a boil over a high heat. Turn off heat, carefully discard the water, and refill with more hot or boiling water or broth. (This process will yield a cleaner broth.) Return to a boil, turn heat down to medium, and let the meat simmer. Skim off any foam that rises on the surface of the water. Cover the pot, and simmer for at least 2 hours.

Meanwhile, prepare the vegetables according to the ingredients list.

When the meat is cooked and falling off the bone, carefully put the meat into a colander, let it cool slightly, and remove the bones. Return the meat to the broth; add cumin and salt and pepper to taste. Add the vegetables, cover, and simmer until they are all soft, about 30 minutes. Add chickpeas, if using, and heat through. Serve with a dollop of sour cream, if desired.

Serves 8

WATERMELON JAM

In Turkmenistan, this is served with tea and bread.

About 3 cups (456 g) watermelon, cut into chunks

2 cups (400 g) sugar

¼ cup (60 milliliters) fresh lemon juice

6 tablespoons (2 packages) powdered pectin ("low sugar" or "no sugar needed")

Remove seeds from the melon, and place flesh in a blender. Puree to yield about 2 cups.

Put the pureed watermelon, lemon juice, and sugar in a pot. Bring to a rolling boil, then reduce heat to simmer.

Carefully whisk in the pectin powder, making sure it doesn't clump.

Bring the jam back to a boil, then reduce heat. Simmer, stirring frequently, for about 20 minutes.

Pour the jam into a glass jar. It will set completely once it has cooled.

The watermelon jam can be canned or stored in the refrigerator for up to one month.

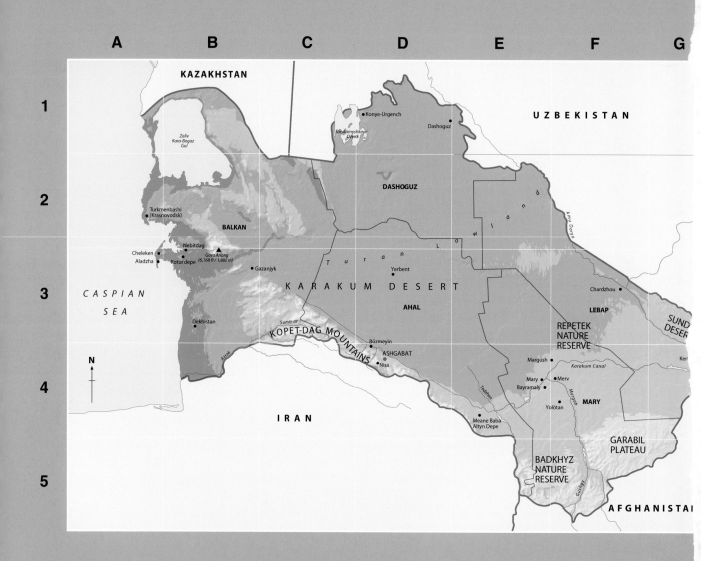

	A	B	C	D	E	F	G

KAZAKHSTAN

1

UZBEKISTAN

• Konye-Urgench

Sarykamyshkoye
Ozero

Dashoguz •

Zaliv
Kara-Bogaz
Gol

2

DASHOGUZ

Turkmenbashi •
(Krasnovodsk)

BALKAN

Nebitdag •
Cheleken •   ▲
Aladzha • Kotur depe •   Gora Arlang
                        (6,168 ft / 1,880 m)   • Gazanjyk

Amu Darya

L o w l a n d

3

*CASPIAN
SEA*

T u r a n

Yerbent •

KARAKUM DESERT

AHAL

Chardzhou •

LEBAP

**SUND
DESER**

Dekhistan •

**REPETEK
NATURE
RESERVE**

Sumbar

KOPET-DAG MOUNTAINS

Büzmeyin •

ASHGABAT
• Nisa

Arrek

Margush •

Karakum Canal

Mary • • Merv
Bayramaly •

Ker

4

N
↑

Tedzhen

Meane Baba
Altyn Depe

Yolötan •

Murgab

MARY

IRAN

**GARABIL
PLATEAU**

5

**BADKHYZ
NATURE
RESERVE**

Gushgy

AFGHANISTAN

MAP OF TURKMENISTAN

G **H**

KAZAKHSTAN

Ozero Aydarkul

TAJIKISTAN

SUNDUKLI DESERT

Gora Ayrıbaba
(10,299 ft / 3,139 m)

Kerki •

Gaurdak •

● Capital city
● Major town
▲ Mountain peak

Feet	Meters
6,600	2,000
3,300	1,000
1,650	500
660	200
0	0
Below	Sea Level

Afghanistan, E5, F5, G4—G5, H4—H5

Ahal, C2—C4, D2—D4, E2—E5

Aladzha, A3

Ashgabat, D4

Badkhyz Nature Reserve, F5

Balkan, A1—A3, B1—B4, C1—C4

Bayramaly, E4

Buzmeyin, D4

Caspian Sea, A1—A4, B2—B4

Chardzhou, F3

Cheleken, A3

Dashoguz City, D1

Dashoguz Province, C1—C2, D1—D2, E1—E3

Dekhistan, B3

Garabil Plateau, F5, G5

Gaurdak, H4

Gazanjyk, B3

Iran, A4—A5, B4—B5, C3—C5, D4—D5, E4—E5

Kara-Bogaz Gol, A1—A2, B1—B2

Karakum Canal, C3, D3—D4, E4, F4, G4

Karakum Desert, B1—B4, C1—C4, D1—D4, E1—E5, F2—F5, G3—G5, H3—H4

Kazakhstan, A1, B1, C1—C2, G1, H1—H2

Kerki, G4

Konye-Urgench, D1

Kopet-Dag mountain range, B3—B4, C3—C4, D3—D4

Koturdepe, B3

Lebap, E2—E3, F2—F4, G3—G4, H3—H4

Margush, F4

Mary City, E4

Mary Province, E3—E5, F3—F5, G4

Meane Baba Altyn Depe, E4

Merv, F4

Murgab River, E4, F4—F5

Nebitdag, B3

Nisa, D4

Repetek Nature Reserve, F3

Sarykamyshkoye Ozero, C1—C2, D1

Sundukli Desert, G3

Tajikistan, H2, H4

Tedzhen River, E4

Turkmenbashi, A2

Uzbekistan, C1—C2, D1, E1—E2, F1—F3, G1—G3, H1—H4,

Yerbent, D3

Yolotan, F4

ECONOMIC TURKMENISTAN

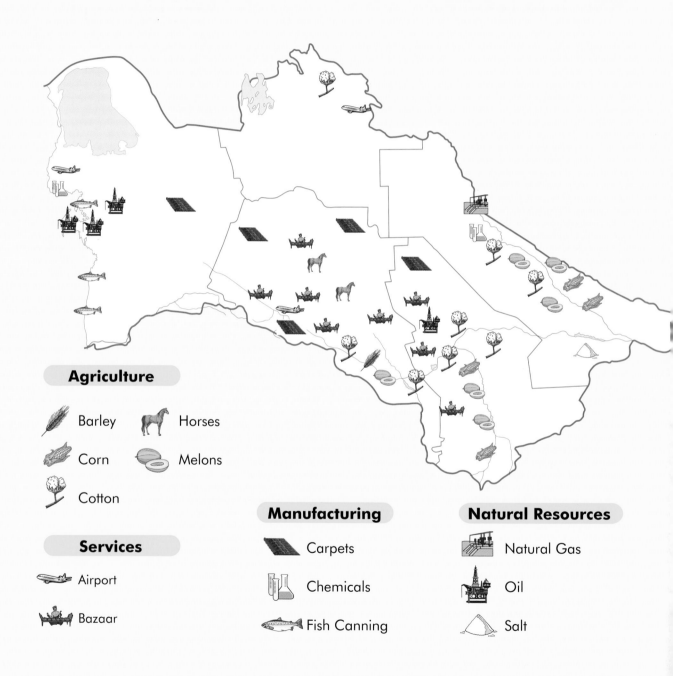

Agriculture

- Barley
- Horses
- Corn
- Melons
- Cotton

Services

- Airport
- Bazaar

Manufacturing

- Carpets
- Chemicals
- Fish Canning

Natural Resources

- Natural Gas
- Oil
- Salt

ABOUT THE ECONOMY

All figures are 2017 estimates unless otherwise noted.

GROSS DOMESTIC PRODUCT (GDP, OFFICIAL EXCHANGE RATE)
$37.93 billion

GDP PER CAPITA (PURCHASING POWER PARITY)
$18,200

GDP BY SECTOR
agriculture: 7.5 percent
industry: 44.8 percent
services: 47.7 percent

NATURAL RESOURCES
petroleum, natural gas, sulfur, salt

AGRICULTURAL PRODUCTS
cotton, grain, melons; livestock

INDUSTRIES
natural gas, oil, petroleum products, textiles, food processing

LABOR FORCE
2.65 million (2019)

CURRENCY
Turkmenistan manat (TMT)
1 manat = 100 tenge

banknotes: 1, 5, 10, 20, 50, 100, 500 manat (no plural form)
coins: 1, 2, 5, 10, 20, 50 tenge; 1, 2 manat
$1 USD = 3.50 TMT (August 2020)

EXPORTS
gas, crude oil, petrochemicals, textiles, cotton fiber

IMPORTS
machinery and equipment, chemicals, foodstuffs

TRADE PARTNERS
China, Turkey, Algeria, Germany, Russia, United States

CULTURAL TURKMENISTAN

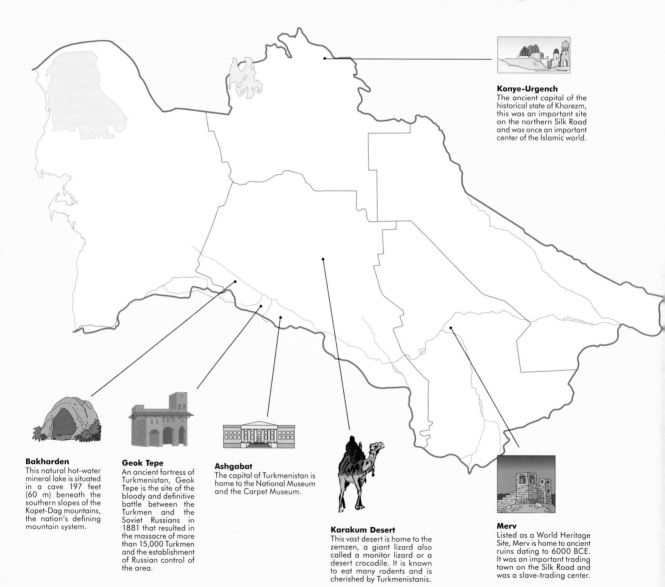

Konye-Urgench
The ancient capital of the historical state of Khorezm, this was an important site on the northern Silk Road and was once an important center of the Islamic world.

Bakharden
This natural hot-water mineral lake is situated in a cave 197 feet (60 m) beneath the southern slopes of the Kopet-Dag mountains, the nation's defining mountain system.

Geok Tepe
An ancient fortress of Turkmenistan, Geok Tepe is the site of the bloody and definitive battle between the Turkmen and the Soviet Russians in 1881 that resulted in the massacre of more than 15,000 Turkmen and the establishment of Russian control of the area.

Ashgabat
The capital of Turkmenistan is home to the National Museum and the Carpet Museum.

Karakum Desert
This vast desert is home to the zemzen, a giant lizard also called a monitor lizard or a desert crocodile. It is known to eat many rodents and is cherished by Turkmenistanis.

Merv
Listed as a World Heritage Site, Merv is home to ancient ruins dating to 6000 BCE. It was an important trading town on the Silk Road and was a slave-trading center.

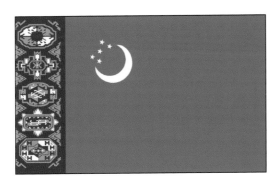

All figures are 2020 estimates unless otherwise noted.

CAPITAL
Ashgabat, population 846,000

POPULATION
5,528,627

POPULATION GROWTH RATE
1.06

ETHNIC GROUPS
Turkmen 85 percent, Uzbek 5 percent, Russian 4 percent, other 6 percent (2003)

LANGUAGES
Turkmen (official) 72 percent, Russian 12 percent, Uzbek 9 percent, others 7 percent

RELIGIONS
Muslim 89 percent, Eastern Orthodox 9 percent, unknown 2 percent

URBANIZATION
urban population: 52.5 percent of total population

BIRTH RATE
18.3 births per 1,000 population

TOTAL FERTILITY RATE
2.04 children born per woman

DEATH RATE
6.1 deaths per 1,000 population

NET MIGRATION RATE
—1.7 migrants per 1,000 population

INFANT MORTALITY RATE
30.8 deaths per 1,000 live births

LIFE EXPECTANCY
total population: 71.3 years
male: 68.2 years
female: 74.5 years

LITERACY RATE
99.7 percent (2015)

TIMELINE

IN TURKMENISTAN	IN THE WORLD
300s BCE	
Alexander the Great conquers Central Asia, including the area of present-day Turkmenistan.	**117 CE**
	The Roman Empire reaches its greatest extent.
600 CE	**600**
Arabs bring Islam to Central Asia.	The height of the Maya civilization is reached.
900	
Ancestors of Turkmen people migrate to the area of present-day Turkmenistan.	**1000**
1200	The Chinese perfect gunpowder and begin to use it in warfare.
Genghis Khan seizes control of parts of Central Asia.	
1400–1800	**1530**
Turkmen are ruled by Persians in the south and Uzbeks in the areas of Khiva and Bukhara.	The transatlantic slave trade begins.
	1558–1603
	The reign of Elizabeth I of England takes place.
	1620
	Pilgrims sail the *Mayflower* to America.
	1776
	The U.S. Declaration of Independence is written.
	1789–1799
	The French Revolution takes place.
	1861
1881	The American Civil War begins.
Russians take over Turkmenistan following the Battle of Geok Tepe, killing 15,000 Turkmen.	**1914–1918**
1921	World War I destroys much of Europe and Russia.
Turkmenistan becomes the Turkmen Soviet Socialist Republic.	**1939–1945**
	World War II devastates Europe and parts of Asia.
	1945
	The North Atlantic Treaty Organization (NATO) is formed.
	1957
	The Russians launch *Sputnik*.
1960s	**1966–1969**
The Turkmen cotton crop becomes central to the Soviet economy, beginning the destruction of the Aral Sea.	The Chinese Cultural Revolution takes place.
	1969
	U.S. astronaut Neil Armstrong becomes the first human on the moon.

IN TURKMENISTAN	IN THE WORLD
1985	
Saparmurat Niyazov becomes leader of the Turkmen Communist Party.	
1991	**1991**
Turkmenistan becomes independent with Niyazov as president.	The Soviet Union breaks up.
1992	
Turkmenistan adopts a constitution.	**1997**
1999	Britain returns Hong Kong to China.
Parliament makes Niyazov president for life.	
2000	
Niyazov publishes the *Ruhnama*.	**2001**
2006	Terrorists attack the United States on September 11.
Niyazov dies of a heart attack.	
2007	
Gurbanguly Berdimuhamedov wins uncontested presidential election.	
2008	**2008**
Berdimuhamedov orders removal of a rotating gold statue of his predecessor in Ashgabat, and a new constitution approved.	Americans elect their first African American president, Barack Obama.
2012	
Berdimuhamedov wins a second term.	
2015	**2015–2016**
Construction begins on a natural gas pipeline from Turkmenistan to India, Pakistan, and Afghanistan.	ISIS launches terror attacks in Belgium and France.
2017	**2017**
Berdimuhamedov gains a third term in office.	Donald Trump becomes U.S. president.
2019	**2019**
Human Rights Watch declares Turkmenistan "one of the world's most closed and repressively governed countries."	President Trump is impeached.
2020	**2020**
Turkmenistan's government denies the existence of COVID-19 within its borders.	The COVID-19 pandemic spreads across the world.

GLOSSARY

Akhal-Teke
The Turkmen horse, a swift, lightweight animal bred to survive the demands of desert life.

Arvana dromedary
A camel with just one hump, also called an Arabian camel.

bakhshi
A shaman or singer/poet.

dograma
A dish of shredded meat and bread.

dutar
A two-stringed lute used in traditional Turkmen music.

felt
A fabric made by matting protein fibers, such as wool or hair, using water, soap, and a great deal of rubbing or rolling.

gul
An eight-sided figure in a variety of designs used to identify a tribe and to decorate its members' belongings. The Turkmen flag displays the gul of the five major Turkmen tribes.

keshme
A felted wool rug or bed covering.

koynek
The traditional Turkmen woman's floor-length dress with elaborate embroidery around the neck.

nomad
A person who moves his or her residence seasonally within a defined area.

plov
A rice dish with meat, fruit, or vegetables.

Ruhnama
The "*Book of the Soul*" written by Turkmenistan's first president, Saparmurat Niyazov.

steppe
A partly or sometimes dry area where grass is the main natural covering.

Turkmenbashi
The name President Saparmurat Niyazov gave himself, meaning "Father (or Leader) of all Turkmen."

yurt
A round tent, framed with lattices and covered in felted wool; a type of residence nomadic Turkmen have lived in for centuries.

FOR FURTHER INFORMATION

BOOKS

Fatland, Erika. *Sovietistan: Travels in Turkmenistan, Kazakhstan, Tajikistan, Kyrgyzstan, and Uzbekistan*. New York, NY: Pegasus Books, 2020.

Lonely Planet Central Asia, 7th edition. Franklin, TN: Lonely Planet Global, Inc., 2018.

The Silk Road, 3rd edition. London, UK: Apa Publications Group, 2017.

ONLINE

BBC News. "Turkmenistan Country Profile." https://www.bbc.com/news/world-asia-16094646.

CIA. *The World Factbook*. "Turkmenistan." https://www.cia.gov/library/publications/the-world-factbook/geos/tx.html.

Encyclopedia Britannica. "Turkmenistan." https://www.britannica.com/place/Turkmenistan.

Eurasianet. Turkmenistan archives. https://eurasianet.org/region/turkmenistan.

Ministry of Foreign Affairs of Turkmenistan. https://www.mfa.gov.tm/en.

New York Times. Turkmenistan archives. https://www.nytimes.com/topic/destination/turkmenistan.

Radio Free Europe/Radio Liberty. Turkmenistan archives. https://www.rferl.org/Turkmenistan.

Turkmen.news. https://en.turkmen.news.

MUSIC

City of Love, Ashgabat. Real World, 2006.

Instrumental Music of Turkmenistan. King Record Co., 2013.

Turkmenistan: Songs of Bakhshi Women. Silex/Auvidis, 2017.

Various artists. *Songs of Turkmenistan*. World Music Library, 2007.

BIBLIOGRAPHY

BBC News. "Turkmenistan Country Profile." https://www.bbc.com/news/world-asia-16094646.

BBC News. "Turkmenistan Profile: Timeline." https://www.bbc.com/news/world-asia-16098048.

Chapman, Wilson. "Ashgabat, Turkmenistan, Is the World's Most Expensive City for Expats." *U.S. News & World Report*, June 18, 2019. https://www.usnews.com/news/cities/articles/2019-06-18/ashgabat-turkmenistan-is-the-worlds-most-expensive-city-for-expats.

CIA. *The World Factbook*. "Turkmenistan." https://www.cia.gov/library/publications/the-world-factbook/geos/tx.html.

Encyclopedia Britannica. "Turkmenistan." https://www.britannica.com/place/Turkmenistan.

Eurasianet. *Akhal-Teke: A Turkmenistan Bulletin.* "Turkmenistan: The Dog Days of August." September 1, 2020. https://eurasianet.org/turkmenistan-the-dog-days-of-august.

Freedom House. "Turkmenistan." https://freedomhouse.org/country/turkmenistan/freedom-world/2020.

Lement, Virginia. "Religion and the Secular State in Turkmenistan." Central Asia-Caucasus Institute and Silk Road Studies Program, June 2020. http://silkroadstudies.org/resources/Religion_and_the_Secular_State_in_Turkmenistan_-_Victoria_Clement_-_10.06.20_-_FINAL_wCover.pdf.

Ministry of Foreign Affairs of Turkmenistan. https://www.mfa.gov.tm/en.

Najibullah, Farangis. "Escape from Turkmenistan: Almost 2 Million Have Fled, But the President Looks the Other Way." Radio Free Europe/Radio Liberty, June 8, 2019. https://www.rferl.org/a/escape-from-turkmenistan-almost-2-million-have-fled-but-the-president-won-t-hear-of-it/29987972.html.

Nunez, Christina. "Q&A: The First-Ever Expedition to Turkmenistan's 'Door to Hell.'" *National Geographic,* July 17, 2014. https://www.nationalgeographic.com/news/energy/2014/07/140716-door-to-hell-darvaza-crater-george-kourounis-expedition/#close.

Pannier, Bruce. "Turkmenistan, a Country for Old Men." Radio Free Europe/Radio Liberty, February 21, 2017. https://www.rferl.org/a/turkmenistan-council-elders-berdymukhammedov-parliament/28322910.html.

Putz, Catherine. "Death and Denial in Turkmenistan." *The Diplomat*, August 19, 2020. https://thediplomat.com/2020/08/death-and-denial-in-turkmenistan.

Robertson Textor, Alex. "What's It Like to Vacation in Authoritarian Turkmenistan?" Adventure.com, July 24, 2018. https://adventure.com/exploring-authoritarian-turkmenistan.

Stronski, Paul. "Turkmenistan at Twenty-Five: The High Price of Authoritarianism." Carnegie Endowment for International Peace, January 30, 2017. https://carnegieendowment.org/2017/01/30/turkmenistan-at-twenty-five-high-price-of-authoritarianism-pub-67839.

Theroux, Paul. "The Golden Man." *The New Yorker*, May 21, 2007. https://www.newyorker.com/magazine/2007/05/28/the-golden-man.

INDEX

INDEX